FIFTY-TWO SUNDAYS

FROM THE PULPIT OF THE PADRE

EDITED BY BARRY D. ROWLAND

T0145468

NATURAL HERITAGE

Fifty-Two Sundays: From the Pulpit of the Padre
Edited by Barry D. Rowland

Published by Natural Heritage/Natural History Inc.
P. O. Box 69, Station H,
Toronto, Ontario M4C 5H7

Design: Derek Chung Tiam Fook
Typography: Video Text Inc.

1st Printing - November 1987

Canadian Cataloguing in Publication Data

Rowland, David Parsons, 1908-1965.
    Fifty-Two Sundays

ISBN 0-920474-46-2

1. Sermons, Canadian (English)*.   2. Presbyterian
Church in Canada — Sermons   3. Presbyterian Church
— Sermons.   I. Rowland, Barry D., 1941-
II. Title.

BX9178.R68F54 1987   252'05271   C87-095233-1

This book is dedicated to my wife, Barbara,
and my children David, Krista, Brian;
my family universal;
to the congregation past and present of
York Memorial Presbyterian Church;
to my mother whose love and devotion inspired this work;
to the memory of family and friends who have fought the good
fight and have finished the course.

CONTENTS

FOREWORD

W. E. Sangster in his book *These Things Abide* tells the story of the scientific lecturer who astounded his audience by putting in a plea for the closed mind. "Not a mind closed by prejudice or by unreasoning preoccupation but a mind that exercises a wise conservatism declining from dashing here and there in pursuit of the fashion of the hour."

Many writers have drawn upon the act of navigation to illustrate our journey through life. A navigator must steer a course by taking a bearing on definite and fixed points. A star does not slip, a lighthouse does not wander, but to take a bearing from a cloud would prove fruitless since it moves, is continually changing shape and with time, disappears.

More than any other time modern life requires us to take a bearing and relate our position to definite points - points based on faith, conviction, commitment.

One need only to glance through the pages of a daily newspaper and listen to television or radio commentary to ascertain that society is finding it increasingly more difficult to maintain some semblance of sanity in the face of despair and disenchantment. When we turn to our institutions for relief we find more often than not that they merely add to the confusion. In too many instances that one institution designed to play a key role, the Church, is not forthcoming with any clear or powerful direction. For some reason there is an unwillingness to take a stand, to preach from a position of personal conviction. Far too often our pulpits have become sounding boards for theories of psychiatry, psychology, sociology and the like. One almost has the feeling that Biblical reference and teaching is viewed as primitive, crude and unacceptable for presentation to a modern congregation. Sadly, the layman in the pew is left unsatisfied, hungry for substance, despondent that the one institution capable of providing the focus is too busy "chasing other windmills".

David Parsons Rowland was a compassionate, caring pastor. He was a man of conviction, deep faith and vision. He practised what he preached, believing that with God all things are possible. He was a man of action, full of enthusiasm, determination, with a great sense of humour. When he put his hand to the plough there was no turning back. Throughout his ministry he preached the Good News, in simple direct terms that afforded the listener a bearing in the struggle to answer those questions of faith, daily living, family, relationships, life as a whole.

Fifty-Two Sundays: From the Pulpit of the Padre is, in part, a response to the many requests for copies of David Rowland's sermons and addresses. Selecting has not been an easy task. The aim is to highlight his philosophy, objectives and beliefs. Faith, conviction and commitment tie the component parts together.

Sermons are meant to be preached. They are designed to influence one's thinking, actions and life. How unfortunate it is that once delivered the tendency is to put them away to gather dust.

If, in fact, sermons have more than transitory value then we have an obligation to preserve them and make them available to those in each generation who, although they may face different problems and struggle with burdens unique to their time, require the same answers.

This book has been designed to complement the reader's religious education. It follows a weekly pattern beginning with the first Sunday in January (The Study of Christian Stewardship).

I trust that each selection, in its own way, will provide food for reflection, a guidepost for living, a bearing to assist us as we navigate our course through the journey of life.

B.D.R.

REVEREND DAVID PARSONS ROWLAND,
M.C., C.D., D.D.

Dr. Rowland was born in Dublin, Ireland in 1908 and came to Canada with his family as a young man. While engaged in a series of manual occupations he heard the call to the Christian ministry. He graduated from Knox College in Toronto in 1935 and was ordained by the Presbytery of Toronto on May 21st, 1935. While attending college he was greatly interested in athletics and played for the Knox College and University of Toronto soccer teams.

While still a student at college he organized a congregation at York in 1934 and was called and inducted as its first minister on June 8th, 1936. In 1938 the first phase of the church building was opened and dedicated. When World War II broke out he resigned from his congregation to accept a commission as chaplain of the Irish Regiment of Canada with which he went overseas and shortly thereafter attained the rank of major. He was decorated with the Military Cross and mentioned in dispatches. When war ceased, he returned from active service and was again called by York Presbyterian Church, the induction taking place on April 4th, 1946. Through his suggestion the name of the congregation was changed from York Presbyterian Church to York Memorial Presbyterian Church as a tribute to Canada's war dead.

Major Rowland continued to take a keen interest in the Irish Regiment and was chaplain of the Peace Unit until the time of his death. He was also chaplain of the Silverthorn Branch 57 of the Royal Canadian Legion and of the 36th Ulster Division, Old Comrades Association. He was very active in the Orange Order, having been Provincial Grand Master for Ontario, Imperial Grand Chaplain of the World and Vice-President of the St. Patrick's Irish Benevolent Association. In addition, he was a member of the Masonic Order. He also served two terms as Deputy Reeve for York Township. For some years he was a member and chairman of the Parole Board of Ontario.

Through his capable and zealous leadership the congregation grew rapidly and the present beautiful church ediface was opened and dedicated on March 9th, 1952. Throughout his ministry he laid emphasis on the youth of the community with the result that his congregation opened and dedicated, in 1957, the Christian Education Building which was named *The David*

Parsons Rowland Youth Centre as a tribute to his excellent leadership and service. The same year Knox College honoured him by conferring on him the degree of Doctor of Divinity honoris causa.

While Dr. Rowland was active in community and fraternal affairs, his congregation and the Presbyterian Church in Canada always had first call upon his time. He served on many boards and committees of the church. He was chairman of the Church's Chaplaincy Committee and also of the Chaplaincy Committee of the Canadian Council of Churches. He was first moderator of the Presbytery of West Toronto.

Dr. David P. Rowland will not soon be forgotten. Wherever his work took him he was always devoted to the cause of Christ whether on the playing field, the battlefield, in the fraternal lodge, council chamber, the congregation or the Church at large. He enlisted the lives and services of men and women in the work of the Kingdom. Multitudes of people can testify that he was behind many of the good things that happened to them. He was an ardent Christian, a wise counsellor, a loyal friend and a kindly pastor.

THE STUDY OF CHRISTIAN STEWARDSHIP

Stewardship is a preaching of the Gospel that involves us, not in pious statements concerning the faith, but in practical commitment of ourselves and the things we possess to Jesus Christ.

Since Christian stewardship is the only practical way that ministers and congregations can become involved in an effective service to Jesus Christ, it becomes fundamentally important that we try to understand its meaning and purpose in our lives. Conditions today dictate a type of action that the Christian and the Christian Church must take to meet the many evils facing humanity. It is time for the Church, without fear or favour, to make her Christian impact on all life. It is only the impact of our Christian faith that can eradicate and remove society's evils.

I see no way of facing these problems unless we become faithful and honest stewards of Jesus. Pious words or zeal for the things of God are certainly not the ammunition that we require to battle the forces that face us. There has to be, on the part of us all, a belief that our faith must be backed up by means to defeat the forces of evil. The day is far gone, if in fact it ever existed, when the Church can stand on a sanctimonious sideline and denounce evil in the hope that it will eventually be removed. We must get into the front line putting on all the Christian equipment that is available and meet the enemy with power and the persuasion of the Gospel. We need to know that the forces of evil are well supplied and well equipped with material things to advance their cause. We must meet the enemy with determination and dedication. Mediocrity within our ranks must go and we must become a well disciplined force of righteousness thoroughly prepared to meet every foe that sets out to destroy the cause of righteousness. If Communism is prepared to spend millions on propaganda it behooves the Church to stop spending nickles.

It is important to emphasize that Christian stewardship is not some new-fangled idea to raise money to meet budgets. Christian stewardship is an attempt to raise new men and women in Christ Jesus who are prepared to commit everything they have and invest it for the cause of their faith and for the honour of their Lord. Service of our fellow man is necessarily accompanied by stewardship of possessions. It is not possible to separate our attitude toward people from our attitude toward things, for if we spend our lives in the service of our fellow man, we will necessarily spend our money in the same cause.

For where your treasure is there will your heart be also.

We cannot respond to God in one of these and not the other. Jesus had more to say about material possessions than about any other subject, for He realized the insidious danger of owning things. The danger in possessions lies in the fact that they are likely to lead us away from God without our even being aware of our disloyalty. We shall substitute means for ends and never know we have done so until we have already been caught up in our materialistic pursuits. To be materialistic is to make our decisions on the basis of money without reference to human need. It is to live as though there was no God.

Jesus used the figure of the steward to describe man's responsibility for material things recognizing that God owns everything and that we hold what we own in trust for God. To be a steward is to administer in the name of the owner, to use the goods for the owner in a manner in which the owner himself would have used them. The steward's responsibility is different from that of a tenant or a renter as the parables of Jesus very clearly show. The tenant, having paid to the landlord a percentage of his profit in return for the use of the property, can use the rest of the profit as he sees fit. It is his as long as he pays his rent. The policies to be followed in earning and spending are of his making and not the landlord's. The steward, on the other hand, represents his overlord in every phase of administration. He does not pay a percentage for use of the land. He is given his living for his service to the owner. The policies are the policies of the owner and the purposes are established by the owner.

It is the Church's belief that we who have heard the call to faith are related to the material things of the world as God's stewards and not as God's tenants or renters. God does not give us a lease on the property we own. He never relinquishes His ownership but retains the full title in His own hands. It is His Kingdom, His business and we are stewards administering for Him.

All that we have is Thine alone, a trust, O Lord, from Thee.

The tithe, which is only one dimension of Christian steward-ship, is often put forward as a fair estimate of man's responsibility to God in the economic realm. It does not, however, represent the Christian's total obligation to God. The Law of the Tenth was an Old Testament law. Unlike other Old Testament laws, it is to be retained by the Christian if he needs such a law for the regulation of his life. It is not to be regarded as an adequate delineation of the Christian responsibility. Christ has set us free from laws except, where in our immaturity and selfishness, we need them. The law of the tithe is regarded by the Christian Church as a beneficial rule designed to help us to determine the portion of our income to be set aside for carrying on activities specifically related to the organized work of the Kingdom of God. This is the one area where every Christian can be effective. Many Christians complain that there are so many things they cannot do. Here is something that all can do and all can practice. Without a rule of this kind, we are likely to overlook God's work because of the immediacy of our own, not willing to acknowledge that God's work is our own.

But the tithe is not the whole responsibility of the Christian steward and the Church has never thought of it as such. We use the word "stewardship" as a definition of our total responsibility in the handling of goods and property. It holds that the principle of stewardship governs the total administration of whatever business we are engaged in or whatever money we possess. These principles refer to all economic transactions of whatever nature: whether production, marketing, consumption; whether in giving or receiving wages; whether in requiring or performing services.

> Because this is my work, O Lord, it must be Thine
> Because it is a human task, it is Divine.

For convenience we have always permitted stewardship to fall under the "three T's" where we describe Christian stewardship in relation to time, talents and treasury. This is the total of a man's life and in this total he is able to give expression to his faith.

Christian stewardship is the practice of systematic and proportionate giving of time, abilities and material possessions based on the conviction that these are a trust from God to be used in His service for the benefit of all mankind. The whole theme of Christian stewardship, as we seek to express it in the life of the Church, is for each of us to recognize that we are recipients of the riches of the providence of God and of the grace of God, and as a result of this we must find ways to express that stewardship in our personal lives.

STANDING BEFORE THE MIRROR OF GOD

I fancy that everyone during the course of a day, has a chance to look in the mirror. This is not a vain thing to do but quite proper and necessary. When you look in the mirror what do you see? The natural reply would be — "I see myself." We would clearly be startled if we saw someone else! Actually, there is someone else. Someone who is very interested in you, interested in not only how you look but also interested in what you think, what you say, what you do. In a way that is what Christian stewardship is all about. It is standing before the Mirror of God, permitting God to interrogate us concerning how we are spending our time, our talents and our treasury, and how we are making God's gifts available to others.

Christian stewardship is an attempt to relate all of life to God, recognizing that God is the giver of all things and out of this knowledge and this experience the Christian is called to return to God that which is His. As far as the Christian is concerned, Christian stewardship for him is found in worshipping, in witnessing, in working, in giving. All these are ours by our Christian experience and out of these must come our response to Almighty God. Unless our faith is part of our life it has no meaning whatsoever. In the days of our Lord upon the earth we find Him looking for performance and not proclamation. The Christian today stands in a world where performance is very essential if we are to meet the total requirements of the Church of the Living God in the world. As we stand before the Mirror of God there are some questions that He would put to us today:

How much of our time are we contributing to advance the spiritual interest of the Christian Church? As a member of the Church how much time do we give in order that the Church and the community might meet every Christian commitment that comes before it?

How are we using our abilities and talents in the work of

the Church — in teaching, leadership and numerous kinds of Christian service? Are we sharing what God has given us so that others might receive a similar blessing or are we hiding our light under a bushel and asking someone else to do that which we ourselves are capable of doing?

How much do we give of our substance for the advancement of the Kingdom of Jesus Christ in the world? Do we just tip God? Do we give when we feel like it or just give when we actually come to church? In other words, God wants to know if we are intelligent givers. Out of all that He has given to us in material things, are we making a return to Him of the tithe which He requires from those who put their trust in Him.

There is no more debatable subject connected with Christian stewardship than the question of tithing. There are those who object to it as legalistic. There are others who insist that it is absolutely binding upon every Christian resting their belief upon the undeniable teaching of Scripture particularly in the Old Testament. Tithers point out that the tithe or tenth is but the beginning of giving. It is not the ceiling of giving it is only the floor. From it the pious Jew advanced to new levels of giving which went far beyond the tenth. On the other hand, there are those who argue that a Christian is not under the Law but under Grace. They insist that Christian giving must not be restricted to the Old Testament principles. It must be the expression of a grateful spirit not bound by legalism.

These are points well taken, however, for a Christian to insist that the tithe is not binding places him under the burden of demonstrating in his giving, that his faith prompts him in many situations, to go beyond the tithe. Objections to the tithe as legalistic should not be used as a smoke-screen. The hard fact is that most Christians and givers, in general, do not begin to approximate a tithe in their giving. It should be pointed out that Jesus recognized the validity and practice of the tithe; that He refused to let it become a substitute for the manifestation of real religion is clear. In the Epistles you will find that when people gave to the Early Church they did not give on the basis of a percentage — they gave everything.

We have recognized through the years the spiritual value of the tithe. We have felt that this is the only way to meet the obligations that are ours. We should point out, too, that as a result of this practice we have freed ourselves from many of the secular means that the Church uses to raise money. One of the great blessings that comes when people tithe is that the relationship to Jesus Christ becomes a very personal thing and they know that in the administration of the resources that God has given to them, they are doing it, not for their own sake, but because they love Him. Tithing is not a compulsion from without; it is an expression of something within. It says, "What shall I render unto the Lord for all His benefits towards me?" It recognizes the importance of some loyal principle in giving and lays hold of the tenth as that principle.

There are three elements that are necessary for a proper understanding of Christian stewardship. The first is that the redeemed man is not his own. He has been bought with a price. Out of that experience or out of that purchase, there must come a gratitude that enables each Christian to respond to God with all that he has so that the total, and I mean everything here, as it relates itself to the Christian advance of Christ's Kingdom, is met out of that commitment. So Christian stewardship, whether it be the giving of our time, our talents or our treasury is an act of faith. This is the one ingredient of our Christian experience that we can express. When this attitude is acknowledged, accepted and practiced, it prevents the Church of Jesus Christ from becoming a beggar or a peddler.

In my ministry I have never made an appeal for finances. I believe that giving is a personal relationship between you and God. If you love Him and want to serve Him then you will give that which you have for Him. It might amaze some people to know that at no time have we sought pledges from our people. You have never been visited to sign a pledge that you would give so much each year. There are those who feel that pledges are necessary for the careless, for the people who apparently require this sort of thing. Be that as it may, we have found our way in the practice of Christian stewardship and it does not follow that direction.

It is important to remember that what you do yourself has an effect upon others. What a great thing it is to say that you are a steward of God. Many people within a congregation are influenced by the witness of those who have faithfully and quietly gone about telling the story of what Christian stewardship has meant in their homes, in their business and in their lives.

STEWARDSHIP MEANS ACCOUNTABILITY

*Moreover it is required in stewards, that a man
be found faithful.* I CORINTHIANS 4:2

Accountability is one of the important phases of Christian stewardship. Accountability is something that is engrained in all of us. Since we are creatures capable of asking and answering questions, we will always be, by nature, a bit inquisitive. Accountability is not a new word or a new term. Each day, each week, each month, each year, we are reminded of its importance. Very soon we will have to give an account to the government of the money we have made, how we spent it and what our return ought to be.

I will never forget my first understanding of the meaning of accountability and the influence it had upon my life. One Saturday morning I left home and did not return until late in the evening. My parents, of course, were quite distressed. I was in no way distressed for I was having a pretty good time. Upon arriving home my mother asked me to give an account of myself. Since my account apparently was not in keeping with her thinking, I found that accountability carried with it some discipline!

In our study of Christian stewardship we have learned that God is the Creator of life and everything in the universe. Man may adapt and alter but he does not create anything. Man is a steward of all he has, or is, or may become, and as a steward man is responsible to God his Creator for life and all its blessings. God and man are made for each other. Man is made in God's image. Man alone of all God's creation can answer His wisdom with understanding, His purpose with co-operation and His love with affectionate response.

With this in mind I want to emphasize a further concept of stewardship. Stewardship hasn't so much to do with possessions as it has with life, and life in order to be lived must be lived through the medium of giving. Therefore, our giving — the amount of it and the spirit of it — is the acid test of our church membership. We may say that we are attached to the Church and that we believe in what it stands for and is seeking to do; however, we spend less on it than we do on luxuries and pleasures. Our profession is out of line with our practice and has little substance to it. There are many people who follow this course. Their giving is occasional, spasmodic, ill-proportioned. It depends on what is left over when the other things have had their full share.

Sometimes it means that all that goes to the Church is the small change lying in our pockets. We may identify this with Christianity but certainly it presents a weak argument. The majority of us are like that. We are so busy furthering our own interests, so attracted by the good things of life, its pleasures and indulgences, that we become self-centred, so unlike Christ, that the art of giving sacrificially is absolutely forgotten.

It is on this basis that we must bear in mind the meaning of accountability. After all, God didn't just give us our life and the things in our life to squander and to waste. He wants us to be reasonable people. He wants us to see that our relationship with Him is not barred by covetousness or by any form of personal indulgences that might separate us from Him. Those who accept Jesus Christ as their Lord or Saviour know that one day they must give an account to Him of how they spent their time, their talents and their material possessions. It was never intended that it should be all spent upon self and the Church today stands in a world of great need. We stand in a community which needs Christian witness, and what we do after all will be more important than what we say. The expression of our faith, love, kindness and generosity will be more important than how accurately we say our prayers, read the Word of God or how well we can preach our sermons.

I make no apology to all who are members of the Church to insist that you have a responsibility here and because you have a responsibility you will be held accountable to Almighty God. Where we are unable to agree on some minor features, there are certainly major directions that must be emphasized and must at all times be observed if we are to call ourselves stewards. We can never forget the fact that life is a trust, an assignment from God and we owe Him an accounting. We brought nothing into this world and we carry nothing out. As good stewards we are expected to account for our holdings and give evidence that we have kept faith with the Lord of Life.

When we reach the end of this journey, it will not matter what we had, it will only matter what we were. Did we understand that we were in debt to life? The great world around us belongs to another, whose we are and to whom we owe both gratitude and allegiance. That after all is the best in life. We know that we are debtors to the Lord of Life. Someone has said that the secret of happiness is in knowing this:

> Only as we live by the law of expenditure do we find our greatest joy,
> Not in getting but in expressing what we are.

There are tides in the ocean of life and what comes in depends upon what goes out. The currents flow inwardly only where there is an outlet. Nature does not give to those who will not spend. Her gifts are loaned to those who will use them. No greater joy awaits us than the joy of living each hour of each day as a sacred trust from God. On that basis the accounting is made easy. Accountability, to have any significance in your life, must be attached to consecration and consecration, as I understand it, is a total commitment of the whole man to his faith. Stewardship must never be simply legalistic nor must it ever put the Church in the position of being a beggar where we use Christian stewardship as an occasion to appeal for money.

If we can see that life is a trust from God, we owe Him an accounting of what we have done with the talents that He has placed in our keeping. Surely this is no time for a sidelong glance. This is no time for arguing about the merits of this thing or that thing. This is not a time to split hairs. This is a time in the name of the Lord, that the Church and her people must come to the place of a deep consecration where we shall put our Lord, His Church and His work first and foremost. We cannot afford to wait until we see what others do with their lives. God is calling us today to make this consecration of ourselves.

> Take my life and let it be,
> Consecrated, Lord to Thee;
> Take myself, and I will be,
> Ever, only, all for Thee.

THE CHALLENGE OF
CHRISTIAN STEWARDSHIP

Whatsoever ye do in word or deed, do all in the name
of the Lord Jesus. COLOSSIANS 3:17

I have no way of assessing the impression that our series on Christian stewardship has left upon your life. I do not know whether you have been moved to surrender your life as a steward to God. Whether you have lit a fire or put out a spark is the critical thing. I can say this, however, that I have never concluded a study in Christian stewardship without some lives being changed. I fervently pray that for the cause of Christ and His Kingdom, we may find within the life of our congregation a deepening of spiritual life and a more holy desire to serve the Lord with all that we have.

There are two misconceptions surrounding Christian steward-ship that I have sought to correct and both of them fall into the category of Christian tithing.

My greatest fear is that people who do not understand the great motive of tithing, that is gratitude to God, are in danger of looking upon it as a money-raising scheme. It is not. Rather, it is a way of teaching us a means to bring us to God. A deepened faith brings home to our hearts the flame of Christ. Stewardship teaches us how to worship by giving ourselves. The man who knows that God is at the centre of his life reveals the daily nearness of God. He sees around him the evidence of God's love and gives himself to God in gratitude as a transformed man. The purpose of tithing is to secure not just the gift but the giver, not just the possessions but the possessor.

My second fear centres around the evil of self-righteousness. I remember a minister calling me about a family, members in this church for several years, who had moved to the other end of the city and became members of his congregation. They, like many others here, were converted to Christian stewardship. They were no time in their new church until they became actively engaged in all its work. The church, however, had run into some financial difficulties and the Board of Managers had placed the problem in the lap of the Women's Association. The women met with the minister and every conceivable suggestion was made to tackle the problem. Then the newest member of the association got up and offered this advice, "If you would practice Christian stewardship and tithing like they do at York Memorial you wouldn't have any financial problems." The minister had called to enquire if what the woman had said was true. Her intentions may have been well meaning, however, what the dear lady had forgotten was that it had taken four years of my preaching to convert her and she was aiming at conversion in five minutes! Always remember the tithe is between the man and his God. I will always challenge you to the gospel of Christian stewardship but in the final analysis the decision must be yours. So long as God knows it, it is not necessary for me or for anyone else to know.

There are three points I want to make in this concluding address and they all relate to the conception of the steward: As a steward you should be challenged with a high standard of Christian service and this Christian service must be directed to the cause of Christ. As a steward I want you to trust Christ with your life. Finally, I want you to accept without fear your Christian freedom as a steward, thus giving you an opportunity to assert your Christian responsibility.

When you became a Christian you immediately became involved in the Kingdom of God. Jesus made it plain that discipleship would cost something and unless a man was willing to pay the price, he could not be a citizen of His Kingdom. He did not call men to ride on a "glory train". He was not a leader of a party that was going to hand out patronage when the party came into power. He would have no honours, luxuries or prestige to offer or favours to bestow upon those who came into His Kingdom. Rather did He call men to self-denial and sacrifice to travail in hardship, to endless service to the losing of their lives. His Kingdom is made up of volunteers. He will never conscript anyone. The Church is but a part of His Kingdom and if you're in it you are called to serve.

> Rise up, O Men of God!
> The Church for you doth wait;
> Her strength unequal to the task,
> Rise up and make her great.

The trusting of Christ with your life is at the very core of Christian stewardship. The Church was started by those who first gave themselves to the Lord. Jesus put it another way when He said,

Seek ye first the Kingdom of God, and His righteousness;
And all these things shall be added unto you.

You are not trusting God with your life if in some area of it you exempt Him. The atheist is sometimes more honest than the Christian — he keeps God out altogether and works at it. The Christian dilemma is that we only let God in where God will not inconvenience us.

I recall the first time I saw the completed plans of this church long before the sod was turned. I remember the architect saying, "This is what it will look like if you follow the plans." I am sure the Great Architect of our life is saying to us, "This is what your life will look like if you will follow My plan", and Christian stewardship is a plan of God. Christian service is not confined to the Church. It has its spring there. I believe Christian service means taking our religious faith and showing what a difference it makes in our daily living. What does it mean to be a Christian? — a Christian judge, a Christian lawyer, a Christian businessman, a Christian trade-unionist. When Christians take the principles of our Lord and apply them in their secular activities, the public will wake up and take notice of them as they did with Peter and John and say, "These men have been with Jesus." The stewardship of service has brought more people into the Kingdom than all the sermons that have ever been preached. Putting your life at the disposal of Christ is your entrance into the Kingdom of God.

I want you to assert your freedom as a steward so that in accepting your responsibility you will be able to render to God that which belongs to Him. The moment you take up this position be ready for opposition. The hour you declare your total allegiance to Christ and in His freedom begin to discharge your responsiblity, be prepared for the slings and arrows that will come. I recall a young man dedicated as a steward of God; he got married and it wasn't too long before his wife was telling him that he was giving too much time and too much money to the Church. It wasn't necessary he was told to go to church every Sunday. Ironically our antagonists are sometimes found within our own household.

There may be many things wrong with the Church and because of its weakness people may treat it in a shabby fashion.

There are many who think that the Church is only interested in money. They treat it, in many ways, like the farmer who complained to his neighbour that he didn't know what he was going to do with his son. It seemed that every time he turned around he wanted money from him. Last month it was $10.00, a few days later it was $15.00, a week ago he wanted another $10.00. Yesterday he had the colossal nerve to ask for $25.00. The neighbour listened to the complaint and said, "What does he do with all that money?". The farmer replied, "Don't know, ain't never given him none yet." All too often the same thing is true of those who complain about the Church asking for money. They don't know what the money is spent on for the simple reason, "They ain't never given her none yet."

God is calling us all to a stewardship today. Are we going to be faithful? The hour for decision is now. Your time, talents and treasury are now before His eyes. Can you lift your eyes from them to Him and say, "Lord what will you have me to do?"

TEACHING IN THE FOOTSTEPS OF CHRIST

Teachers and preachers alike need the stimulus that comes to us from the Christian work that we do. Sometimes, however, as we journey along in our tasks, the wells dry up and we feel that we have reached the end of the way. At times like this we must come back to the source of our inspiration and try to find in the Scriptures the strength and purpose that leads us to do what we do. In the four Gospels, Jesus Christ stands out as the perfect example; the matchless leader; the Redeemer who gave Himself for us; the Saviour who frees men from the power of evil; the King of Kings and Lord of Lords.

His favourite title seems to have been "Master" which means teacher. How many times are we told that "Jesus taught them". He opened His mouth and taught them. He taught them in the synagogue. He taught them by the seaside. He sat in a boat and taught them. He went up into a mountain and taught them. He taught them many things in parables. He taught them not as a

Scribe but as one having authority and first hand knowledge. He was always teaching people something.

What was His teaching like? It surely had these three qualities. First of all it was interesting. Secondly, it was concrete. Thirdly, it was positive.

First of all it was interesting. People liked it. The common people heard Him gladly. They followed Him from one town to another to hear more of it. It got hold of them. Roman soldiers said of Him, "Never man spake like this man." Jewish Rabbis, keen on form, said, "How knoweth this man letters, never having attended schools?" There was a charm and a finish about it that appealed to them. That outdoor crowd on the hill listened to Him until He had finished His Sermon on the Mount. They went away saying, "His word was with power."

He laid hold of His hearers and lodged His truth in their minds to stay. He wrote nothing Himself. All that we have has come down to us through the memories of those who heard Him say it. If it had not been interesting they would not have remembered it. The Master's teaching was interesting and those who heard it retained it in their minds.

Many books have been written about Jesus and about the Gospels. It will take less than one hundred years for them to be forgotten. One hundred years from now the four Gospels — Matthew, Mark, Luke and John — will continue to be read. They will not be forgotten. They are interesting, arresting, vital.

As teachers you too must be interesting if you are to be remembered. No one can afford to be dull with children because they themselves are full of interest. They are always looking for something to startle them, to catch their imagination and the more we can bring before their minds the great truths of the Bible the more will they remember these things.

Reflect upon the lesson of the Samaritan woman at the well. Here are two people so far apart at first. He was a Jew, she was a Samaritan. Jews had no dealings with the Samaritans. He was sinless, she was openly immoral, living at that time with a man who was not her husband. The only thing they seemed to have in common was the fact that they were both thirsty. The Master then began on a bit of common ground by saying to her, when He saw her filling her water pot, "Give me a drink." Presently, growing out of their conversation He went on to say, "Drink of this water and you will thirst again. Drink of the living water that I give you and you will never thirst."

The Jews worshipped in Jerusalem. The Samaritans on Mount Gerizim which rose before them as they stood by the well. The place does not matter. God is Spirit. Worship Him anywhere in spirit and truth for the Father seeketh such to worship Him. He continued to converse until the woman actually forgot what she had come for. She left her water pot, the account says, and went back to the little town saying to everyone she met,

> Come, see a man, which told me all the things
> that ever I did: is not this the Christ?

Soon the field was filled with people coming out to hear such teaching. It got hold of them. The record says that many of the Samaritans also believed on Him. How fresh and stimulating the whole chapter is. I have never read it over without getting a fresh thrill. There is not a dull line in it. Here was the Master teaching!

His teaching was also concrete rather than abstract. Abstract means literally drawn away from life. His teaching was saturated with life. The whole method, for example, of Incarnation as we hold it, lies embedded in the principle of making the truth concrete rather than abstract. What does it mean to be neighbourly? A lawyer asked, "and who is my neighbour?" He thought that by shrewd cross-examination he could discredit the Master's teaching. Jesus replied, "A certain man . . .", and went on to tell the story of the Good Samaritan. How much more effective that concrete picture is than some long learned discussion of the moral imperative of the altruistic attitude in society. Some wise sociologist might talk for an hour in words of five syllables about how social action should be motivated or how philanthropy should be evaluated, without getting anywhere. The parable of the Good Samaritan has in it only one hundred and sixty-five words. One can repeat the whole of it in sixty seconds yet how it covers the ground! It really leaves nothing more to be said about duty or about the general concept of being neighbourly. That picture will hang there before the eyes of the world and the eyes of children as long as the world exists. His teaching is concrete.

Reflect upon the Sermon on the Mount. It is profound. It goes clear to the root of the matter, yet there is scarcely a word in it that a ten year old boy cannot pronounce, spell and understand.

Brief though it is, it has in it fifty-six clear cut metaphors — word pictures, thumbnail sketches, brief etchings of the truth. For example; salt, light, lilies, moth, rust, beam, bread, stone, fish, scorpion — some fifty-six of the them.

One could read the entire Sermon on the Mount, as reported in the Gospel in fifteen minutes. His teachings were always vivid and picturesque. He made His truths stand up like a rabbit's ears above the grass of a meadow. It is this concreteness that is important in our teaching and in our preaching. Unfortunately our pulpits suffer from the lack of it. How often after a sermon have you heard people say, "It went right over my head." You could never say that about the teaching ministry of Jesus — it not only went into the head but into the heart. As teachers we must realize that when we take care to develop our presentations in a concrete and understandable manner we will reach any group under our charge.

Finally, His teaching was positive. It was devoid of doubts, denials, uncertainties and prohibitions. He never wasted His breath telling people about things that were not so. His first great command, "Thou shalt love the Lord thy God with all thy heart", and the second which is like unto it, "Thou shalt love thy neighbour", are both positive.

He never stood first on one foot and then the other, talking now out of the right side of His mouth and now out of the left side as if He could not quite make up His mind. It may be so and then again it may not! We cannot be sure! There is a good deal to be said on both sides! Perhaps the truth lies half way between the claim that there is a God and that there is not! Like a certain philosopher who is forever trying to carry the particular brand of spring water on both shoulders — he never gets anywhere. In his long drawn out debate he uses up much of the English language but is never able to say anything positive.

You never get that kind of "fog and mist" in the Master's teaching. No halting between two opinions. His "yea" was a yea and His "nay" a nay.

> Ask and you will receive.
> Seek and you will find.
> Knock and the door will be open into the unseen.
> I am the way, the truth and the light.

Ye shall know the truth and the truth shall make you free.
Come unto Me all ye that labour and are heavy laden,
Take My yoke upon you.
Link up your life with Mine for the drawing of the common load.
Learn of Me the meaning of life.
Ye shall find rest to your souls for My yoke is kindly.

Is there anything else in print so straightforward and constructive. When He came to place His appraisal upon goodness He emphasized the positive rather than the negative. He knew that it is what a man does rather than what he refrains from doing that gives him character.

We often hear it said of some inoffensive person who has just gone to his reward, "Oh, he was such a good man. He never drank. He never smoked. He never swore or gambled. He never said an unkind word about anybody." He may have been all that. His whole life may have been as harmless as rainwater but what did he do? How far did his life count for righteousness? For a more equitable industrial system in the world? For honest politics in his home town? For better educational facilities for the underprivileged? For improved sanitary conditions in the poorer sections of the city? What did he do for his church and his fellow man? When people simply refrain, their goodness speedily becomes weak, thin and dull.

The Master said that it is positive goodness which marks a man up on the books which the Lord keeps. When we study the four Gospels we find that His most pungent warnings were directed not against the courser sins of the flesh, bad as they are, but against the sins of neglect. They had to do with the things which people leave undone. The man in the parable who failed to use his one talent did not do anything wrong with it. He just wrapped it up in a napkin and buried it in the ground where it did not harm anybody.

The five young women at the wedding, the Foolish Virgins they are called, failed to have their lamps lit. They did not go out and stone the wedding procession or say nasty things about the bride or anything of that sort. They simply failed as light bearers when the bridegroom came because their lamps had gone out and they had no oil in their vessels.

The rich man who failed to receive the sufferer at his own

gate did not go out and abuse the poor fellow, he just let him starve to death.

> Inasmuch as ye did it not to the least of these,
> the hungry and the sick, the lonely and the imprisoned,
> the struggling and the destitute, ye did it not to Me.

> Not everyone who says to Me, Lord, Lord, shall enter the
> Kingdom of Heaven but he that doeth the will of My Father.
> If you know these things happy are ye if you do them.

As teachers we must covet the best. We may not always get it but we can want it earnestly and persistently. In that quest for the best we cannot do better as the heralds of a Divine Gospel or as plain everyday Christians, than to follow closely the Master whose teachings were always interesting, concrete and positive. To whom shall we go? He has the words of Eternal Life. May the Spirit of the Lord be upon us anointing us to teach the Good Tidings to those who sit before us and to bring to bear the light of Jesus Christ upon their lives.

As teachers we must follow the example of our Lord and of our Saviour. As we have seen He had a clear-cut definite message. It was a message from the Heart of God to the soul of man. It was a competent, adequate message — a lamp unto our feet and a light unto our path. It made men wise and furnished them with motives, stimulus and guidance for all good work.

There is nothing that will help us more in our teaching ministry then to walk with Christ and to listen to Him as He makes His appeal. He never set out to win arguments. His main objective was to win men and women to His Kingdom and to His side. Surely this is the very thing that motivates us in all that we do for our Lord.

I trust that what I have said will bring to your life and to your teachings some inspiration. You play an important role in this part of God's vineyard. The boys and girls that are ours today are going to be the men and women of tomorrow. If only now we can sow the seed of the Kingdom of God in their lives, how richer and fuller will be their lives and the lives of the people of the community.

Therefore, no matter what be your task on Sunday or during the week whether it is teaching, leading, keeping a role or gathering a collection, you must learn that all these things have a bearing upon the advancement of the child in the Christian way. I do not say that there will not be times when you will be discouraged, but in that hour lean heavily upon the Master who said, "I will never leave thee nor forsake thee."

So to your task with new vigor, fresh devotion and with a deeper dedication to Christ. Let us set our hands that we may raise up a community of righteousness bearing witness to what we have done on behalf of Jesus Christ.

DYNAMIC RELIGION

But let judgment run down as waters, and righteousness as a mighty stream. AMOS 5:24

The plea of the prophet reaches us today with searching and challenging emphasis. His people, the Lord's elect, had fallen morally and spiritually into the pit of inaction and moral degradation. They had permitted religion to become a "rubber stamp" and had closed their hearts and heads to vital spiritualized renewal. In their prosperity they had forgotten God and in their delight at the things of the world they had forsaken the Covenant of God. Israel had gone to sleep religiously and in her smug complacency had left behind the heights of her religious attainment. A wall had been built between themselves and God and in this state of spiritual inaction, their moral life became dulled and their spiritual life full of apathy.

The prophet was not an alarmist nor was he a busybody. His words and his message were after all to be taken seriously but no one had ears to hear. The king, the priest and the nation wrote him off as a "crackpot". He was going around finding a fly in everyone's porridge! He was making the good in the nation look very, very bad. Rather than attacking their own moral inaptitude, they attacked their prophet. They belittled him. They made him look ridiculous.

In our own day and in our own world we find a parallel —

a parallel, of course, that is quite alarming and disturbing to every prophet of God. A determined world-wide attack is being waged against the faith and morals upon which Christian civilization has been built. I am not referring here to the advance of Communism, although no one but a fool would ignore its power or the godless core of its ideology. I think rather of the equally ruthless and less honest materialism that is gaining control in those countries, which for centuries have called themselves Christian.

Events in our own land should call the Christian Church and Christian people to give ear to the words of the prophet. Scandals involving political leaders have shaken the confidence and conscience of the land. The standards which generations of loyal and patriotic men and women have regarded as helpful, are now set aside as irrelevant, unimportant or even worthy of contempt. Conversely, what generations of loyal men and women have held as unhealthy and destructive to character of family and nation has been whitewashed as progressive.

The only way I know that we can meet the indifference of the age — this superficiality of form and religion — is by bringing the dynamic religion of Jesus Christ to bear not only upon the Church but also upon the nation. In fact this marks the difference between Christ and the Pharisees. They were interested in the letter of the law and Christ was interested neither in the letter or the law, but in life. He was interested not in how life could serve law but in how law could serve life. He was concerned that all human life spread roots into God, cast off its self-made chains and attain both spiritual and material abundance. Like the prophet, Christ was a radical and yet it is only with the dynamic of a radical religion that we can get to the root of all evil and obliterate it from our world.

You say to me, "What can I do about it? I am just a lowly individual. I'm just a citizen. I'm just a working man with very little influence." If you are a member of the Christian Church you can make your presence felt. The tendency today is for many of us to go along for the ride without sharing the load. A few weeks ago I was in High Park and noticed some boys using a toboggan. As they were pulling it up the hill, one of the lads said to another, "Unless you pull you won't get a ride." I think the same can be said of many Christian people. Too few of us are doing the pulling and too many of us are just riding. The Church and the pew, the pulpit and the nation must meet the tasks and with Christ's Gospel, address the healing of the nation.

The dynamic Christian is a front line soldier. The static Christian is a home base operator. The dynamic Christian is always on the firing line. The static Christian is the man with the desk job far removed from conflict, controversy and growth. The dynamic Christian is a pioneer. The static Christian a recluse. The dynamic Christian is not afraid of risk, adventure, creation. The static Christian loves nothing so much as safety, security and peace. The static Christian is afraid of new ideas. The dynamic Christian is afraid of the lack of one. We need more men like Amos in our pulpits today. Men of courage. Amos saw beyond the world of Hebrew society. He saw God — the God of all the earth. The God whose righteous will is creative justice for the enemy as well as the ally, for the poor as well as the privileged.

Martin Luther, too, was a radical. A dynamic Christian. He struck a blow for new and better days. He rebuked the greed of the Church and the state. He saw God, the God of all the earth, whose love was made flesh in Jesus, whose spirit moved beyond our society to a wider and wiser world. With one blow he demolished salvation by graft, indulgences, magic spells and rituals. He set his face toward the city of sanity, the city of tomorrow, the city of God.

We, too, must catch the spirit in a day when the nation and the world needs the Christian faith. We need once more a true investment of our stewardship if we are really to do something to change the world in which we live. We need to take this religion, whose praises we sing on Sunday, and make use of it each day we live and mingle with our fellow man. The human need about us is great, it cannot be met unless we give this truth to men everywhere.

Let judgment run down as waters, and
righteousness as a mighty stream.

There are one or two steps that we can take. First of all we can meet every problem in the nation, in society, at home and in the Church in the name of Christ. This, of course, is not the safe thing to do. It is not the popular thing to do because we are always fighting against a wicked and well mechanized enemy.

I remember during the war a Dutch underground worker

saying to me, "We did not win major battles. At best we were a thorn in the side of an all powerful wrong. We resisted what was neither true nor sane and died in our cause." The Dutch underground did not win the war. It was nonetheless on the side of human liberty and human sanity that finally prevailed against military might.

I believe the Church has got to stop being a "caged parrot", just mumbling secular words and pious phrases. We need to become "eagles" that will mount upon high and go out across our world determined to change that which needs changing and bring to life that which is dead. We need to be concerned, as Christ's children, with the absolute rule of His way of life in words and deeds. I believe a changed life is more eloquent than a multitude of pious sermons. Like the prophet and like all men who have volunteered to follow Jesus, we must stand for Him. No miracle will be achieved in the nation or in the Church, until we learn the genius of His leadership and the hope of our own.

THE RELIGION OF INFORMALITY

Now when the even was come, He sat down with the twelve.
MATTHEW 26:20

This day in the life of Jesus had been hard. It was filled with conspiracy and betrayal, yet in the midst of the storm the Master found time to sit down with His little band of followers. In this act He was revealing to them that His assurance is more important than the uncertainty that is found in the evil perpetrations of men. The disciples were being introduced to a situation that was difficult for them to understand and assess, for after all they were human and the ills that had entered into the little camp must have had a profound effect upon their lives. We do not have a complete record of all that was said on this occasion but enough is there for us to know that without this pause for personal instruction, these men could not go through the storm nor could they retain their personal faith in Jesus Christ.

It is difficult to assess the mind and the emotions of Jesus and His disciples at this time. When the storms of opposition are howling and raging like uncontrolled fire, when treachery of the worst kind is shaping and sharpening its spears, it must have been a relief for the little band to move from the terror of opposition into the quiet lagoon of peace and quietness and listen, with unruffled tension, to the words of their Lord. It is the informality of the occasion that brings its blessing and imposes its own tranquility.

In our busy life as Christians, we have lost the art of taking time to sit down with our Master and bring to Him the needs of our heart and our lives. The act of worship should always be an occasion when we as disciples sit down with Him. Many problems of the Church and moral dilemmas that beset men and women, could be resolved if only we would take time to sit down with Jesus. Let us, therefore, enter reverently into the circle of His presence that we too might learn afresh that He has the answer to our needs, to our frustrations, and to all the difficulties that beset us in our lives.

The first lesson that the disciples learn is that the Living Christ is always meeting us in a great act of friendship. No matter where we move in the Gospels, we will always observe that Jesus never sought to win men by arguments or by reason and logic. He was never interested in what men thought about Him or even what they believed themselves. He reached them at the place where they could understand Him and in that understanding He developed a common friendship. He never seemed to be too careful about the tags that men wore — whether they belonged to this or to that organization. As a matter of fact, He was continually criticized for mingling with publicans and sinners, yet He replied,

They that are whole need not of a physician,
but they that are sick. I came not to call the
righteous but sinners to repentance.

The friendship of Jesus had nothing whatsoever to do with systems but rather with individuals. He was always seeking men where men could be found. It wasn't the ninety-nine that were safe, that were secure, but it was that one sinner out in the barren places of life that needed the touch of His hand, the lift of His countenance and the strength of His friendship. Having assured them of His undying friendship, He was ready to bestow upon them the act of a new confidence. You cannot have confidence without friendship and Jesus was anxious that His little band would not only see the necessity of having confidence in Him but confidence in themselves. One day they must walk the path alone; must face a common duty alone; must bring to bear the Gospel that He had taught them alone, but with the assurance of His confidence that they could go forward in faith to conquer and bring to all segments of humanity the truth about Him — a truth that would change their hearts as it would change their day.

Many people today have lost confidence in themselves. They have lost confidence in their fellow man. They have lost confidence even in the Church. The Prodigal Son, in whatever generation he might be found, discovered that from a friendship once known there came that hour of confidence when he would leave his sin and return to his father's house. Our greatest need today is to have confidence in the Redeeming Power of Christ and to believe that God in Christ is still revealing Himself personally to us. As we wait before Him in prayer and in His word, He is there to bring to us, and to the broken places of our lives, new structures that will steady us in the storm showing us a better way along which we can travel. A new sea upon which we can sail in confidence towards a new harbour.

There are legions today who have confidence in Christ, for they have learned from experience that only in Him has life purpose, meaning and understanding. If we are in pieces today it is because we have lost the confidence of His presence. We need to sit down with Him, that our faith might be restored and our love invigorated by His gracious spirit.

Friendship and confidence were not the only ingredients present on this occasion. There came to the lives of these men an indwelling of His presence that enabled them to make a personal commitment of themselves to Christ. Surely they had learned with Paul and with Nicodemus.

If any man be in Christ, he is a new creature.

We too must learn that in this commitment we are involved in self-denial, not an easy word; self-discipline, not too easy to accept; and self-surrender which we always find most difficult. But if victory is to come to our lives and in this victory we are to know ourselves as creatures of Jesus Christ, then we too must sit with Him and learn of Him, that the way to true Christian discipleship is by denial, discipline and self-surrender.

This is the foundation of our faith and without it our faith cannot have aim or purpose. We shall discover, as we sit with Him, that there are results that will come, to gladden the heart and bring us peace. This does not exempt us from a service that is demanding; from a discipline that is exacting; from a crusade that will demand our very all.

I implore you to sit this day in His presence and learn anew of His will for your life.

A MAN OF GOD

There are two avenues open for a discussion of the phrase, A Man of God. It might be applied to the man who is merely used by God or it can refer to the man who actually belongs to God. While there is much that would be common to both these lines of interpretation, there is also much that is widely divergent. Many of the most sinful men have been employed in the Divine Economy and often without knowing it. Little did Nero realize that his cruelty converted others to kindness. Little did Rip Van Winkle guess that his habits of drinking turned others to sobriety. Little did Shylock dream that his stinginess only served to make others more benevolent. Little did Benedict Arnold surmise that his betrayal of home and country aroused others to patriotism. Little did Voltaire suspect that his atheism kindled for others the joy of belief.

God can utilize any man for His glory and give wisdom to the wise, even through the lips of the foolish. The man who is used to the best advantage in the Kingdom is the man who, through faith, belongs to God, who has come to love the Lord with all his heart, mind and soul and who consciously serves Him and seeks daily to do His will.

In picturing a man of God one imagines a servant like John or Moses who has matured with the years and grown mellow in the nearer and sweeter presence of God. Spiritual life is a growth, a continuous progression towards a heavenly ideal. The very first glance at such a life arrests us and wins our approbation. The believer, of course, shares much with the unbeliever, yet there is something which sets them strangely apart. We can never conceive of the man of God as being childish, sentimental or erratic. There is something about him that is unique and sublime. His character bears the insignia of health, strength and beauty. There is a harmony in his movements; a firmness in his step; a dignity in his bearing; a flush in his cheek; a tenderness in his eye, and in his voice the music of a love divine. He needs no trumpet to announce his coming, no herald to proclaim his virtue, no choir to sing his praise. He comes among us transfigured in the dawn and moves to and fro amid the avenues of need to succour and to bless.

Being a man of God, he is all for God. His speech, his acts, his gifts, his sympathies, his business, his associations, show clearly that he is concerned entirely about the glory of the Father. No selfish interest prompts him; no mercenary motive stirs him; no yearning for fame propels him; no craving for applause causes him to lose his equilibrium. His one aim is to serve the Lord and he does it with gladness. He feels that he is no longer his own — that he has been bought with an awful price. His disposition therefore is generous. There is with him no choosing of the Plains of Sodom; no hiding of gold in a sack; no lifting of stones to hurl at the sinner; no burying of talents in the ground.

Freely he has received and hence he is ready to freely give. He does unto others as they should do unto him. He lends to the poor, remembering that his wealth is a trust. He forgives his neighbours as God in Christ hath forgiven him. He seeks out the lost, rejoicing that he himself has been found. The man of God knows that he has been called to be a messenger of mercy, priest of pity and an ambassador of love.

His temper is valiant. It glows with that determination which fears no principalities and shrinks not from death. Time and time again he is challenged by a Pharaoh or a Goliath or an Ahab but takes the gauntlet in his teeth and promptly decides the issue. He believes that liberty is vital, that truth must reign and that everywhere righteousness should prevail. He stands out courageously as the champion of the individual, the home, society and the state. The hypocrisy of religion knows the fury of his wrath and the corruption of politics shares the cut of his sword. He has no ground to give when honour is at stake. He has no compromise to offer when principle is involved. He has no excuse to plead when duty calls. He is always ready to storm the ramparts of evil and strive for the advancement of all that is good.

Through it all the man of God is reverential in manner. His judgment is not only tempered with mercy, it is refined and strengthened by an active sense of worship. The things around him are immensely sacred. He cannot hear the warbling of the birds in the trees; he cannot watch the drift of a cloud in the sky; he cannot scent the fragrance of the flowers in the garden; he cannot listen to the babbling brook at his feet; he cannot touch a human hand or look into a human face without feeling that the Lord of all is near. He moves among the things that breathe out eternal meanings and that wear the garments of beauty that fade not away. In the myriad wonders of earth, sea and sky and in the midst of the varying circumstances of men and women where battles are fought and victories are won, the man of God is sure to pause and bow the head knowing that the ground whereon he treads is holy.

He is distinguished for his spirit of devotion. In every environment and in all conditions he kneels at the altar to pray. If the winds should blow in the valley of his wandering; if the sunbeams should dance in the glens of his pleasure; if the darkness should gather in the chamber of his dwelling; if death should appear in the very midst of life, the man of God never fails to find comfort in the language and spirit of prayer.

One might conclude that such a portrait of the man of God is a fantasy of the imagination — that its colouring is far too heavenly; that it has no real counterpart among the things of earth. Reflect on the life of Moses. Think of the glory of that character who held his struggling and complaining people in unity for forty years. Think of the magnificence of that purpose which opened wide the heavy gates in the House of Bondage. Think of the grandeur of that self-sacrifice which was offered humbly in a howling wilderness. Think of the splendor of that fortitude which was seen in Egypt, at Sinai and within sight of the Promise Land. Think of that majesty, of that reverence which was visible by the Red Sea. Think of the charm of those invocations which were voiced amid idolatry, in the Tabernacle and beside the tent of Aaron.

Many other consecrated lives have been set in the same rich and fadeless hues: Joseph, Daniel, Constantine and Tertullian. I would whisper to you the prayer of Stephen, "Lord lay not this sin to their charge." I would let you hear again the words of the Earl of Norton by the grave of John Knox, "He lies here who never feared the face of man." I would help you to catch afresh the cry of Latimer, as the flames leapt about him, "Play the man Master Ridley, we shall this day light such a candle by God's grace that shall never be put out." I would have you watch once more John Brown kissing the little black baby as it nestled in its mother's arms on his way to the scaffold, then mounting the steps to die with thanksgiving on his lips that he was counted worthy to suffer for such a cause. I would like you to read with new zeal the story of Livingstone, pouring out the treasures of his life in the burning waste of Africa. Of Gordon standing loyally at his post in the shadows of far away Khartoum. Of Jesus bearing the pain and shame of the Cross for the sin of the world. What shade could be too delicate; what tone too glorious; what background too luminous for the canvas of men like that!

I just wonder if the Divine Artist will need all that wealth of material when He comes to paint your portrait and mine. I wonder if we have so lived or that we shall so live in righteousness that coming generations will rejoice to find our tombstones bearing the epitaph, A Man of God.

ETHICS AND THE ROLE OF
THE CLERGY IN PUBLIC LIFE

We must commend and support every effort that seeks to improve the ethics of men and women in public life. The wrongs that surface are not new. They do, however, place a stigma on those who serve in public life today and act as a deterrent to others who are competent to serve but refuse simply because they do not wish to be tarred and smeared. The whole of political life in this country has suffered from the public indictment of gain and not service. How often have you heard it said of someone in public office that, "He would not be there unless he was getting something out of it."

A code of ethics would simply be a way of teaching men and women in public office that the ultimate and paramount duty of those who serve is to enrich and enhance public office by faithfully putting something into it. The ethics we are after can well be missed by those who demand it simply because they are starting at the wrong place. It should be enunciated again and again that the moral ethic of a nation is vested in the homes of the nation. If we would stop teaching our children about the virtues of right and left and start teaching them the moral implications of right and wrong, it would go a long way to cure the ills of political corruption. I venture to say if our children in our schools were asked to learn the Ten Commandments, or the Sermon on the Mount, which are the basis of all moral ethics and law, there would be those who would cry out discrimination from the house tops!

Physically our diet has a lot to do with our proportions. Our moral diet has everything to do with our personal integrity. There is a feeling today that the foundations of our moral order are shaken and that political corruption has made goodness negative and vice a virtue. Some of the noise is sensational and produces more wind than sail. Our thinking is badly blurred if we imagine that what we are seeing and hearing today regarding the breakdown of public morality is new.

> I know how many are your transgressions
> and how great are your sins.
> You who forget the rights,
> who take a bribe and turn aside the
> needy at the gate.

This statement sounds like something we have read in our daily newspaper, yet this was the condition in 6 B.C.! This only confirms that evil, like righteousness, is not something new. The one place where the problems of right or wrong can be adequately solved is in the conscience of men. Conscience alone has the faculty to distinguish between right and wrong.

There are always two ways open before us and it is conscience that enables us to make the choice. A code of ethics can only function properly at the will of the conscience. It is disturbing when one hears people comment that politics is always a dirty business. If that were so we would not today enjoy such democratic advantages as we now possess — advantages that have been won on the field of honour and human sacrifice. If politics is muddied it is because the citizens of a municipality or country are content to let it be so. Unless we can arouse in the public a sense of their responsibility, there is little we can do to further the cause of ethics in public life.

Unfortunately, there are some who believe that public responsibility, although desirable, must be limited. I am referring to those people who believe that the clergy, for example, have no right to enter public life. There are people who believe that public office belongs to the politicians and not the ministry. Many believe that a clergyman can do a better job on the sideline — be a spectator rather than a participant. As a pastor I am daily involved in the moral and ethical welfare of my community. Anything or anyone seeking to destroy what I am trying to build up, of necessity, must feel the sting of my reproach, either by word or presence.

There are those who believe that your prestige and dignity will be destroyed in the community. I am not too sure what people mean by prestige and dignity. I only hope my life and work in this community has a better foundation than dignity and prestige. These are transitory things. They are not abiding. They are like the wind that comes and goes.

Many people conceive of the Church as a museum piece, set in the community to be looked at, to be revered, to be guarded and to be kept unsoiled. The minister becomes a curator of this ancient relic. I must say that neither the minister nor the Church belongs in this category. We belong to a militant band who in their day turned the world upside down socially, religiously, politically and ethically. We must know that where there is wrong that needs righting, the Church and her clergy will and must intervene.

Already you have heard that as a minister of the Gospel I have not the time to carry on an additional political responsibility. I would like to point out that many of the people who speak about my time in relationship to this community are very often the people who use my time. I have allowed my ministry to serve all people in this community regardless of their affiliation. Many that I have served have no affiliation whatsoever with the Church. I bury their dead. I visit their sick. I assist them with their domestic problems. I go to jails and courts on behalf of their sons and daughters. I help in procuring pensions for them. I baptize and marry their children. I find them work. I give them letters of reference. My door and my church is always open to all faiths.

What I am in effect saying is that nothing in this world can be accomplished without assistance. I will never neglect my Christian responsibility to my church and my youth centre and if the electorate sees fit to place me in office, I will be diligent in the discharge of my duty on their behalf.

A PLEA FOR WISDOM

The fear of the Lord is the beginning of wisdom. PROVERBS 9:10

Throughout the Book of Proverbs the major theme is that of wisdom. Wisdom here is the paramount thing. "Get it", the author says, "and with it get understanding". But what is wisdom? How does it come? What is its source?

To begin with, wisdom is not the same thing as knowledge. One may have a great deal of knowledge but be woefully lacking in wisdom. Our knowledge, for example, of the universe and its laws; our knowledge of science and all its fields; our knowledge in many other human endeavours far exceeds that of Abraham, Solomon, Plato and Shakespeare. But who would dare claim that we are wiser than these men? I think it was Tennyson who said, "Knowledge goes but wisdom tarries." We have all known people who are able in the field of knowledge but whose judgment in the affairs of the world and its people appears to be adolescent. By the same token we have known individuals devoid of formal education who possess a wisdom that brings a great deal of enlightenment.

Wisdom has its source in human life. The wise man is the man who recognizes the important things in life. The things that lead to peace and that sense of wholeness of being really one with the universe. The wise man, the wise group, the wise nation, are those who insist that order has purpose and gives not only direction but a reverent sense of discipline to life. Knowledge can produce a program but it takes wisdom to direct it. Knowledge can manufacture the key but it takes wisdom to open the door.

We send our children to high school and university to fill them to overflowing with all manner of knowledge but when they graduate are they wise? On leaving the institutions of learning, are they ready to grapple with the social and moral dilemmas of life that seem to elude the academic calendar. It was Huxley who said,

> Many of those who are able to stay the course of an academic education emerge from the ordeal either as parrots, gabbling super formulas which they really do not understand; as specialists knowing everything about one subject and taking no interest in anything else; or finally as intellectuals theoretically knowledgeable about everything but hopelessly inept in the affairs of ordinary life. They have no integrating principle in terms of which they can assist and give significance to such knowledge as they may subsequently acquire.

Knowledge by itself is not the true staff of life. It might provide a living but not a life. It may enable us to detect the difference between left and right but it is only wisdom that enables us to detect the difference between right and wrong. We need to see the necessity of having roots as well as branches. Depth as well as height. Wisdom moves us from the general to the particular, from the abstract to the absolute. It is on this foundation we must learn to build our lives. Only then will our systems be right.

> The fear of the Lord is the beginning of wisdom.

Fear here means reverence, awe, trust, a sense of responsibility. Without this God-consciousness in life, there can be no greatness and without this foundation we cannot build.

The aim and purpose of wisdom is to give dignity to personality and direction to all human behaviour. It perceives righteousness in every cause and gives integrity to every labour. It saturates life with love and refuses to sit on the seat of reason counting the cost. Wisdom never analyzes nor does it put tags on men and women. It aims to accept before it denounces. Knowledge, on the other hand, cannot help men until it has them well documented. Knowledge must put them in the right category before it can bring forth its recommendations. Wisdom feeds the hungry then preaches to them. It never asks for a case history before it renders genuine service. Wisdom enters into the depth of a man's thoughts, desires, hopes and aspirations and calls for the homage of his whole manhood. Wisdom puts love at the centre of life. It refuses to bend to the whims and fancies, prejudices and hatreds of prevailing winds. Indeed, it is a well from which the refreshing streams of kindness, goodwill and charity daily come. It bends to the lowest. It administers to the vilest. It declares that in man, most ignorant and depraved, there is something worth saving. In the most wicked of outcasts it sees a possible saint.

In the midst of all our culture and knowledge, this is the ground that should be cultivated. Wisdom, you see, does not deal with facts and figures. It deals with persons. It does not ask if you have a bank account but it does ask if you are an accountable person. Not what you have been or what you are, but what you are destined to become. This is a worthy thought and should not be lost sight of in the complexity of a society where knowledge tends to encourage snobbery and debase human dignity. These are the standards of human conduct that endure. These are the virtues that make men and nations.

Finally, we need to recognize as citizens of a free country that the wisdom of God exercised by men in public life, and in all areas of human involvement, is our best guarantee for the stability of the people of the world. Our Lord told a parable on wisdom. It is the story of two men who built a house. One man built his house on the sand and the other on a rock. Jesus said that the man who built his house on the rock was a wise man.

You will understand that building on a rock involved a great deal of labour, patience and toil and there is no other way that has yet been conceived whereby men can obtain the wisdom necessary to build. The man who built on the rock was building not for today or for tomorrow. He was building for eternity. The man who built on the sand was building for today, for show. He was only concerned with appearance. This could well be a commentary upon our thinking and acting in the twentieth century. Knowledge, as you know, is always rushing us through school but wisdom tarries. The great things in life are not accomplished by shortcuts and very often it requires time to mold men for wise leadership, training and the necessary stability to carry through. A nation without wisdom is like a sailing ship without a sail. We have been fortunate over the centuries that we have had an opportunity to build upon the Christian and democratic way of life. We are, if you like, the spiritual dividends of the labour of faithful men and women whom we call our pioneers.

The complexity of the world in which we live demands that we search our hearts before we give direction, that we train for endurance before we enter the battle. As leaders our task must surely be the making of citizens. The men and women, and I believe they are in the minority, who rant and rave about certain things that happen within the realm of religion and education are not the people we can rely on to advance any cause. Few of these people have ever built our schools, our colleges, our universities, our hospitals or any of our institutions. They are great to pull down but they are not so earnest in building up. Our nation under God and the wisdom that He has to offer for those who seek it and use it should be our earnest goal.

It is still one of the most paramount truths that it is righteousness and God's wisdom that exalteth the nation. Surely this should be the possession of the mother in the home, the father at the office, the farmer in the field, the teacher in the classroom, the libertine and the lawyer, the soldier and the slave. My plea, then, is for wisdom that will enable us to do our duty and not avoid it. To stand by those enduring principles of true religion that came to us in the Incarnate Christ.

SOUL WINNING

I will make you fishers of men. MATTHEW 4:19

There is no more important Christian work than that which is described in our text. Ofttimes we forget the importance that Christ attached to the personal winning of souls. I feel for those who are attempting the winning of souls. We come to realize that such a work is not the easiest. The wonder of it all is that God can do so much with such inadequate implements. I know that we are apt to become dissatisfied with the way that we present Christ to those who we want to win for Him. At best we are all blunderers and indeed insufficient for the Divine task that has come to us.

But since soul winning is that which lies closest to the heart of Christ and is the very heart and expression of the Gospel itself, it behooves all of us who are seeking to follow our Master to know that our main business is the bringing of souls to Him. I feel that there is a needed emphasis to be placed upon this important work within the Church today. If we are not winning souls for Christ we are not fulfilling our Christian mission. I believe that much of our failure in this important work is due to the lack of good spiritual equipment.

"I will make you fishers of men", implies first of all that fishing for men is just as fine an art as fishing for fish. In making this comparison I hope that it may catch some spiritual truth that will enable us to see the vital need of good honest inquiry.

If textbooks could make good fisherman, I feel convinced that I should be one of the best in the country. I have followed a good many hints and theories that I have found in books on fishing, yet when it comes to the practical handling of a rod I am far inferior to those who are poor at the game! In fishing we are all good theorists. Is it not here then, that we should consider this important work of Christ? Books cannot make us soul winners. We may find hints and helpful suggestions in them. They may teach us how to prepare sermons and Sunday School lessons but they have nothing to do with the creation of prophets or spiritual gifts.

We are made by Christ. What we are and what we are destined to become depends on our submissiveness to Him. "I will make you", are His words to His followers. Every useful and fruitful gift is borne directly in His presence. No one else and nothing else can do it. Neither books, friends nor institutions can do it.

I will make you.

While this promise involves the giving of spiritual power, Christ does not exclude in it the man himself. Our Lord expects us to use our mind and allow it to be developed under the influence of His Spirit. He expects that we give His grace the wisest and sanest expression. He demands that the instrument through which

He works should be the best in body, mind and personality.

I often wonder how Christ can work through some of us at all. We see so many today who call themselves Christians going about as if the whole world was "hanging upon the end of their chin". Others give the impression that this world is so corrupt and godless that nothing can be done about it. Some are lazy and do not want to exert themselves for the cause of the Kingdom. Then there are those whose very appearance and conduct drive people away from Christ. Finally, there is the Christian who is so busy putting himself in the limelight that Christ never gets a chance to be front and centre.

The fisherman follows three important rules for successful fishing. Keep yourself out of sight. Keep yourself further out of sight. Keep yourself even further out of sight. Let the trout see the fisherman and he will catch no trout!

There is a lesson here that applies to the art of fishing for men. The preacher needs to know how to keep himself out of his sermon. I know how easy it is to come to the pulpit and make our own little bits of wisdom shine as if they were the be all and end all. We are prone to push ourselves to the forefront of our work in quest of fame, praise and glory. Ego pushes us forward and steals in upon our labour, making us feel that we are so important. To fail would be the end of some noble cause. What we really need to do is keep out of sight. We need to draw ourselves aside and hide in the garments of the Master. Let us ever and always remember that as soon as men and women see us and hear us they will not take our bait. Christ must have sensed this weakness in man when He said, "Open your mouth and I will fill it." This is the essential ingredient in the winning of souls. Let Christ be seen and let Him be heard then the soul will be won.

Let the man who fishes be cheerful. When the fisherman is depressed he cannot throw a line. When his spirits are light he can touch the surface of the water without causing a ripple. This can well be applied in our efforts to catch men for God. If we come before people with a depressed mind and a sad countenance, we lack the ability to throw. If we are heavy in body and mind we will catch no fish. It will be necessary for us to resort to the garments of praise. If we are coming with Good News, it is a contradiction to our faith if we come in sadness. Be sure that you address your approach with praise and thanksgiving.

Good fishermen study the fish. We have often sat beside men who have been catching fish all around us while we have empty hooks. Often our predicament is found in the kind of bait we are using. We are surprised when we are told that the bait we have been using successfully in other places does not work in these waters.

So it is in fishing for men. We need to study them and know the kind of bait that is necessary to catch them. All men cannot be caught by the same bait. We must study the individual, his habits and his tastes. We must discover what will catch this man, that man, and address ourselves accordingly. Remember what Paul has to say on the matter, "To the Jews I became as a Jew that I might gain the Jews." He became all things to all men that he might gain some. He baited his hook according to the fish he wanted to catch. That is what we must learn to do. Bringing our friends to hear a sermon may not effect our purpose. Perhaps a letter will have much better results. Sometimes a direct conversation will constrain one to become a Christian. In other circumstances approaching a person in an indirect way and dropping a word here and a hint there, will achieve the purpose. One word spoken with feeling and sincerity may win a soul for Christ. We must learn to study the person that we are seeking for the Master.

The important thing of all is to keep our equipment in good repair. We must resort continually to the Throne of Grace and leave ourselves in the care of Christ Himself. It is He who will make us fishers of men. Catch one fish and know the thrill of it, and you will always be a fisherman. Catch one soul for God and you will not be satisfied until you have caught many more.

To this work Christians are called. Many of us would not be here today had it not been that someone caught us for Christ. Let us return to our Lord this day for renewed strength to do His work and work His will that many may be brought into the Kingdom.

AN ADVENTURE OF FAITH

He went out, not knowing whither he went. HEBREWS 11:8

There are two worlds in which all men live. One is the world of reason and the other the world of faith. It is not always easy to separate them and because of that they are not the simplest concepts to discuss. The things that we see and can handle or the things that we call tangible are for us, all the more easily accepted and the more readily understood. But when we come to speak of faith or reason we move into an invisible realm and must content ourselves with the evidence that these things produce. We cannot speak of faith or reason as that possessing material qualities. While they may and do operate in material things, we cannot point to the object in which they may operate and say, "That is faith" and "That is reason". For example, your presence tonight in this place is the result of a purpose. You have a reason for being here or you are here because of faith. I have not seen the purpose of your reason nor the purpose of your faith. Neither have you. But I do see the evidence for it when I look at you. The fact that you are here proves that while we may not be able to see and handle faith and reason we can behold them at work.

Because I wish to speak of faith I am not going to enter into a long discussion about the relationship of faith to reason. Such discussions have been going on for a few hundred years and I don't intend to keep you that long! When we speak of reason we speak of that which belongs to man, that which possesses human qualities. It has no place in it for Divine intervention and it refuses to accept anything in terms of faith. In other words, it refuses to believe in anything except what it can see for itself. It always demands proof. Reason never gets above the human element of life.

Faith, on the other hand, has Divine qualities. It is always God-prompted, God-inspired and directed. It does not refuse to acknowledge the powers of reason, rather it takes them and turns them into channels of usefulness and service.

Many of us would have to admit that much of our Christianity is nothing more than a blind unreal acceptance of the faith that comes from God. There is a tremendous uncertainty about our relationship with God. One day we feel that we live in His holy presence while at other times we feel that our belief is nothing more than empty notions. Frankly, that can only be our experience if we see nothing more in our religion than sentiment and emotion that may come to us in the presence of worship. I want to call you to higher heights and to tell you that we must get hold of a believing faith. The Christian Church will fail to make any mark in the world until it begins to live in itself, the faith that prompts the children of God to greater things.

He went out, not knowing whither he went.

This is what I call an adventure of faith. In that text we are reminded that faith produces passion. God takes these lives of ours and fills them so full of His spirit that they become vessels overflowing in our personal service to Him and our fellow men. When God calls as He did to Abraham there must be a complete abandonment of self and all that surrounds self, if we in faith would take up the call and go where He wants us to go and do what He wants us to do. The faith of God then fills our life with passion. When it starts to interpret itself, this passion finds us venturing out as did the early disciples to seek the lost and bring them to the feet of our Lord.

This is the faith that we need in these days and this is the faith that the Church somehow has not been showing. We have not been venturing for God. We have been looking to our own ends and calling upon everyone else, save God, to help.

This attitude must change before God can honour us with His real presence. Where there is passion there is always conviction. There is nothing in this world that we can compare to Christian conviction. Nothing has ever been accomplished where men have lacked conviction.

I am aware of the indifference that asserts itself today. We hear it said that one religion is just as good as another. We are told not to send missionaries to far away lands. The religion of these distant lands is just as good as Christianity. This attitude is assumed to be a virtue and bears the marks of a broad tolerant spirit. In my view this is not the mark of an open mind — it is the mark of an empty mind.

A man who has no passion has no conviction. Where there is no conviction there is no belief. It is faith in God that produces the passion — that gives birth to conviction and supplies force and driving power to life. According to your faith be it unto you. The man who has no faith, no passion, no strong conviction, is useless to his church and to the Kingdom of God. Let us be men and women who listen to the call of God and on hearing it go forth with a faith that leads us to do great and noble things in His name.

Through the ages this call of God has sounded in the hearts of men.

> Whom shall I send,
> and who will go for us.

"I will", said Abraham, and went out not knowing where he went. "I will", said Moses, and smashed the tyranny of Pharaoh. "I will", said Gideon, and waved the blazing torch of freedom for Israel. "I will", said Elijah, and put an end to the idolatry of Baalism. "I will", said Isaiah, and delivered a message which has thrilled each generation. "I will", said Peter, and proclaimed the Gospel at Pentecost that brought three thousand to their knees. "I will", said Paul, and flashed the light of truth into every part of the Roman Empire." "I will", said Savonarola, Luther, Livingstone, Wesley, Lincoln, Booth and countless others, famous and unknown, learned and unlettered, in prominent places and obscure. All these had a personal faith in God and a passion for their fellow men.

God is just as truly calling you and me today. He needs men and women of faith who will be willing to allow Him to lead.

Do not comfort yourself in the fact that all is done that needs doing for the bringing in of the Kingdom. We have heard that from many within the Church. Such an attitude creates a narrow, shallow, spiritual outlook on life that leads to gross selfishness on the part of Christians.

Many of the world's ills today could have been avoided if the Christians of the world had kept themselves close to God and followed where He wanted to lead. We do not need more government, more common international understandings, more laws, more armies. Our immediate need is for more God-directed, God-controlled men and women. Get men to God, call upon men to live by God, to work for God, to believe in God, to follow God and I believe we have found the solution to our world's present needs. Can we afford to stay outside His love and grace any longer?

He is calling to you now. I cannot say where He is going to lead you but I do know this, that His way is the way of life and all who walk in it are led into a fuller knowledge of His love.

God is calling His church today to go forth and follow Him. If you would redeem the world, you must break with it. If the lost are to be saved, you must go out and compel them to come to Him. That is what the call of God means. I know that we try to escape the urgency of that call by saying that such a work belongs to someone else, that our organization doesn't go about things in that way, that our standard of theology is not conducive to such a work.

The day for such pussy-footing in the Christian Church is gone. The hour for casting such religious pride overboard is at hand. The moment for listening to the voice of our Lord is with us. How much better it is to obey Him than listen to the sound of our own chorus. Venture His way today and you will be blessed.

TAKING INVENTORY

Ye did run well; who did hinder you. GALATIANS 5:7

One of the tasks that irritates all businessmen is the taking of inventory. If only they could run their business without this tedious responsibility there might be more blue in their sky. Nonetheless, their progress or decline is vested in this wise and meticulous task. They know that to survive it has to be done and it's a wise businessman who does it with care.

From such an inventory a businessman learns many things. He learns first of all, if he is a success. He learns which commodities attract or do not attract his customers. He discovers if his stock is fresh or stale. He learns if he is losing or attracting customers. If he discovers that he is failing, he sets himself to find out why and endeavours to do something about it. If he discovers he is succeeding, he puts all he has into further improving his position. An inventory is a useful guide and the man of wisdom pays careful attention to its signs.

It was a similar scenario that moved Paul to utter the words, "Ye did run well; who did hinder you". When this church, this people were converted to Christianity through the preaching of Paul, they became a success, spiritually. They rose to the challenge of the Gospel with zeal and diligence. The fire that the Gospel had kindled in their hearts warmed them to deep devotion and unswerving loyalty to Christ. Their beginning was full of hope. Here was a people strong in their passion for the advancement of Christ's Kingdom. Having set them on the right road, with the persuasive passion of the Gospel in their hearts, Paul went on in his Gospel mission.

In the interval something happened. Others followed Paul and preached another gospel. It was the gospel of the law. They began to tell these Christians that they needed something more than Christ to assure them of their salvation. The people listened. They became luke-warm. They permitted other things to come between themselves and Christ. The hard core of personal conviction had now become soft and meaningless. The gladdening experience of regeneration had now become a mournful tune. Where only there was the song of grace, now could be heard the dirge of listlessness. The bright morning of their conversion had turned into night.

If this was the predicament of the First Century Church how much more is it the predicament of the twentieth century institution. Let us as a church stand before the enquiry of our text,

Ye did run well; who did hinder you.

It is not uncommon that we find ourselves at sea as far as our faith is concerned. Much of our Christian thinking has been upset and the measures we once used to guide our Christian calling are strangely absent. Corruption, godlessness, vice and doubt seem to receive all the rewards. Honesty, truth and virtue pay the penalties. There is an attempt to write off Christian belief and conviction, to put it aside as having no meaning in the lives of men and women.

If carelessness and the events in life have affected your Christian attitude, I want in His name to say that you can still run well. Let us remove the hindrances and get on with the march! Let us close our ranks that we can stand firm against every invader that would destroy our faith and bring to naught the sufficiency of Christ.

How do we go about doing this? First of all we must take inventory. Where do we stand? How do we stand? For what do we stand? Where are we in our individual lives so far as Christ is concerned? Is our belief in Him vital, dynamic? Does it find expression in our daily lives or is it something passive and superficial — something we exhibit on special occasions and then wrap carefully away until the next appropriate time? Is our faith conviction or conversation? Is it a flame or a flare? Is it a daring enterprise fraught with risks or a comfortable formalism without strain? Is it a positive force that enables us to stand for something or is it so negative that the only response we make is in the form of indifference?

Are we to be numbered today with those in so much conflict that they do not know what they believe? What the first Christians needed is our need as well. It is first of all a need of the heart.

If thou shall confess with thy mouth
the Lord Jesus, and believe in thy heart
that God hath raised Him from the dead,
thou shalt be saved.

Here we are coming to personal grips with Christ. Here is Christ coming in all His saving power to make of us new creatures. This is the only experience, the only faith, that will get us anywhere. This is the only area where revival can begin. The odds were against Christ in His time and the odds will be against us too. But as His power, His life, His salvation has matched every century and brought it the only satisfaction and the only life worthwhile, it will do the same for us. Our allegiance to Him today will make tomorrow's world yearn for Him.

It is this spiritual rebirth in our lives that will remove all hindrances and put us on the road to Christian living, Christian attainment and bring fresh hope to our distraught world. When we are able to show others what He has done for us, Christ will bring another spiritual awakening to our world.

I am not asking for something that is easy to do. Christ never did. His convictions brought to Him the Cross. Our Christian convictions will also bring us into conflict but it will keep us on the road to righteousness.

If God be for us, who can be against.

With that as our spur, defeat is impossible.

Following this personal decision and building up our spiritual bank will, of necessity, bring to the Church the fires of another Reformation. When man rediscovers himself as the child of God, he immediately sets himself to the task of making the House of God vital in his life and the life of his family. Christ will become a person not a creed. Deeds and not dogmas will be our concern. The Bible, not tradition, will be our authority. Christ, the Head of the Church, will become an absolute and not a fanciful abstraction.

Here is the dynamic that will make the Church militant, a fighting force against the potential of evil in the world. With such a spiritual resolution in our hearts, the self-satisfaction that has caused us to drag our feet, will disappear. We will become a concerned congregation once again. Our stewardship for Christ, which has not touched all our hearts, will have new meaning. When He takes control of us every muscle will be strained in His service. Somehow I know that our religion will mean something more than merely "pew sitting". We will use this hour to garner our spiritual ammunition for tomorrow's labour.

How are you going to answer the challenge of our text, "Ye did run well; who did hinder you"?

This calls for a personal faith in Christ. A fresh devotion to His Church, a concern for the recapturing of our nation for righteousness. This is Christ's program for us. It is immense. It is challenging. You will have to make decisions even though you haven't all the answers. When these times come, you will have to look into the face of Christ and say, "All right, I don't know what to do nor where to go. It's up to you. Take me over for I need you."

> The Old Man of the Earth stooped over the floor
> of the cave, raised a huge stone and left it leaning.
> It disclosed a Great Hope that went plumb down.
> "This is the way", He said,
> "But there are no stairs", said the stone.
> "You must throw yourself in", said the Old Man,
> "There is no other way."

There is no other name given among men whereby they can be redeemed, save Jesus Christ. Will you throw yourself into Him today?

THE LAMENT OF JESUS

and when He was come near, He beheld the city, and wept over it. LUKE 19:41

Palm Sunday inaugurates the final stage in our Lord's sacrificial journey. The scenes and events that appear on the Scripture records of our Lord's last days, leave their own impressions upon the human mind and conscience. There is one scene among many that somehow reveals the very heart of Christ. It is found in the words of our text, "And when he was come near he beheld the city, and wept over it."

Our Lord does not look upon the city as would a military general whose army has been sent out ahead to bring the enemy under submission. The general would delight in his conquer and his army would ravage in their victory. When our Lord looked upon the city, He was seeing much that brought joy to His heart. This was His city. It was composed of His people and He knew His people. Here, was the centre of all customs. Here, too, was the centre of religion, where for centuries all had come to fulfil their religious obligations.

Jerusalem was a landmark in the lives of its people. But Jesus knew more than the human eye could see and the mind comprehend. Here was a city that would resist His love and spurn His Gospel. Here was a city, on the one hand, that would acclaim Him King and on the other deny Him; a city that would praise Him and yet a city that would denounce Him; a city that would lift their hosannas and at the same time defame His name.

On this occasion, our Lord walked into the enemy camp. He did it knowing full well that He was marked for death. He was a young man. His ministry was short. "And when he was come near, he beheld the city and wept over it." We know that there are many things that cause people to weep: sorrow, joy, hurt, restored entanglements, the mending of broken friendships. It was none of these things that caused our Lord to weep. He looked not only at the city but at its heart and at the heart of its people.

Jesus saw a city condemned because of lost privileges. If any people, any nation, any city had a priority on religion, it was this city and this people. It was to them that God had sent the leaders and the prophets. Their whole history was steeped in religion and the hope of the Messiah. It was to them the Incarnation was first revealed and to them the Gospel was first preached. Theirs was a privilege unknown to any other people. We are told He came unto His own.

Privileges are not rights. Hence that which was theirs was passed on to others. We, too, must ask, What are the thoughts of Christ as He looks upon His Church in the world today? What does He see? What should He see? We, too, can lose our Christian privileges by apathy, indifference and carelessness. The things that we take for granted — an open church, an open Bible, the right to worship according to the dictates of our heart — these are privileges but only privileges so long as they are used and maintained. Every time we absent ourselves from public worship; every time we stop reading the Bible; every time we stop saying our prayers; every time, when by our indifference, we stop practicing our faith we are in danger of giving ground to the enemy and losing those high spiritual privileges that have come to us by way of tremendous sacrifice.

There is something else that caused our Lord to weep. He was very conscious of the lost opportunities of His people. I remember an inmate in one of our reformatories saying to me that he had "lots of opportunities but had fouled them up". He had no one to blame but himself. Surely this is an indictment that could be directed against Jerusalem and its people. They "fouled up" their opportunity to know Christ as King and to proclaim Him as their Saviour. When they should have been pursuing a straight course to Him, they were following the devices of their own heart and looking only for an excuse to avoid His challenge. When the day of their salvation arrived, they were found playing hide-and-seek with their religion. When you do that, hate and malice are sure to enter in and there can be no room left in your heart for the Lord.

Opportunities are scarce in our lives. Very often many of us act in this respect like the Prodigal Son. He had the opportunity to be a faithful son and strong citizen and yet he followed the dictates of his own desires which led him out into the far off country. There are many people like him today who know all about the Gospel story. They have heard it preached from our pulpits, seen it acted out in the lives of Godly men and women, but with all that they are still unsaved. They cannot meet the challenge of Christ. They refuse His Gospel. They are always looking for an opportunity to settle the welfare of their soul with Him. Like Felix of old, they are waiting for a convenient season. How often that convenient season never arrives!

"Today if you will hear my voice, harden not your hearts." Instead of tears of sorrow, tears of joy should come to the eyes of our Lord.

Finally, I believe our Saviour wept over Jerusalem because of its lostness. We know that He came to seek and to save that which was lost. Here was a people that did not want to be saved. They refused to accept the message that was His, a message that would change their character and give new destiny to their lives. In the eyes of Jesus, it was their souls that counted most. He craved that more than anything else. He was the answer to their sin and their sinning. Still they persisted in listening to the enemy. That which could have been theirs, by Divine Providence, was spurned. Rather than accept Him as their Lord and Saviour, rather than turn their souls over to His care and keeping, they joined those who put Him to His death and caused His deepest sorrow.

When Jesus looks at us, our lostness is His concern. He sees us not as successful men and women with a multitude of material possessions but rather as men and women who are in constant need of Divine help. Jesus knows that the greatest possession that we can return unto Him is our soul. This is the part of our life He seeks to save. This is the part of our life that possesses immortality.

When the challenge of the Lenten Season comes, we are reminded that here once more is the Lamb of God who has come to take away the sin of the world, pleading with us, who are His children, to be more faithful in our Christian living and pleading with us as lost souls, to turn ourselves over to Him.

Looking, as He does today, upon your life and upon mine

what is there in it that might cause Him to weep? Is it our indifference? Is it our unwillingness to harken unto His voice? Is it our desire to run our own show unaided by Divine guidance? Let not this Lenten Season pass without coming to grips with Him. Turn not your backs for the day of your salvation is now. He calls and in His calling there is redemption for all who will answer Him.

EASTER TRIUMPH

and behold there was a great earthquake: for the angel of the Lord descended from heaven and came and rolled back the stone from the door and sat upon it. MATTHEW 28:2

The Easter story always stirs our hearts. It calls to our remembrance a multitude of experiences that we have passed through and it never fails to confirm our hope or to bring us peace. There would be little comfort in the Gospels if the chapter on the Resurrection was missing. A Gospel that ended on the bloody heights of Calvary would leave us with a dead Christ and it is only a living Christ that can keep the pulse of our soul in motion. It might be sufficient to show how Jesus lived, suffered and died but that would leave us with a dead Christ and it is only a living Christ that can move us into new life and bring to us new hope.

The central fact of our Christian faith is in the Resurrection. This was something that had never happened before in the wise economy of God and would never happen again. The Resurrection marks the beginning of the Christian era and brings to us a new understanding of the power of a living and abiding God. It is the message of the Resurrection that has challenged and quickened the whole world to new life and to new Christian endeavour. Wherever we see any evidence of good in our world, you can be sure that it had its beginnings, its origins, in the Resurrection.

and behold there was a great earthquake: for the angel of the Lord descended from heaven, and came and rolled back the stone from the door.

This suggests the beginning of a new life for men. Here the relationship between God and man is forever settled. Just as the sin of the world paved the way to Calvary, so the Empty Tomb leads us into a fuller and greater life in Him. There are three kinds of people for whom this triumphant Resurrection has a message. The people I refer to are the least, the last and the lost.

Who first of all are the least? To what group do they belong? Sometimes we call them the nobodies in our world, the no-goods, the do-nothings. They are usually the little people. The people who cannot solve their own problems without help. The people who are always going off the track. The people who cause constant consternation to the society in which they live. The only time they hit the headlines is when they are before the courts of the land. They have never been able to avoid the stigma of not being wanted. They lack culture, courtesy and in their own way, they lack all the positive virtues of life.

These people are not new to the world. They have been with us from the very beginning. No matter where we move in our world, we are sure to run into them. But if we have no love in our hearts, the Resurrection comes to their rescue. Christ sees in them rough jewels that can be fashioned into diamonds. They may be the discards of our society, of our families but they are still children of God and as such they are the concern of the Master.

You will recall that even in His day He was criticized not for mixing with the righteous but for mingling with publicans and sinners. But He rose from the dead, that these unwanted people might become for Him the wanted. When our Lord desired to express the greatness of His Kingdom, He said, "The kingdom of heaven is like unto a mustard seed", which is indeed the least of all seeds but when it is grown it is the greatest.

The Gospel of the Resurrection has a message for the last. These are the folk who go into all the races but they never win. They never have any trophies to adorn their mantle. They enter every contest but they are always last. If there is a lineup for some important event you will find them at the end of the line. They are a poor lot. By our standard they are not going to amount to anything. You wouldn't bet on them. You wouldn't trust them with any responsibility. They are always running but never arriving. Always weaving but producing no web. Their lives seem to lack a shuttle and the driving power. You couldn't count on them.

These are the very people for whom the Resurrection of our Lord took place. Jesus saw in this individual the person He wanted to assist, to love and redeem. He gave them hope because He gave them direction. He said on one occasion, "Many that are first shall be last and the last shall be first." This was the impetus that these people needed. Many of them because they believed in Jesus, went out and extended His Kingdom among men. Never measure a man because he appears to be last in every enterprise. Always remember that when the last are touched by the life of Christ they become the very first in His Kingdom.

The final type for whom the Resurrection has some meaning is the lost. The men and women who have lost their way in life. They have lost life's dream and ideals. They lack a principle and they lack understanding. They go with the crowd. They are the pawns of every exploiter. They are usually regarded as the dregs of society. But Jesus, looking out upon the lost, had this great word to say, "For the Son of man has come to save that which is lost, I come not to call the righteous but sinners to repent."

These are the basic truths of the Resurrection. They grip us with a freshness as they touch us with a new hope. This truth lightens our darkness and enables us to see that the work we are called to do in the Church, in our organizations and in the world has real meaning when Christ is our motivating power. We miss the gladness of this great day simply because we become too self-indulgent. We need to hear the great words of the apostle Paul. "Tis no longer I who live but Christ who liveth in me." Here, you see is a transfer of authority — not me but Christ runs my life. Hence we need to submerge all the selfish motives that prompt us so that we, with these lives that God has given us, may bring succour to a suffering world removing its hate and hostility and enabling men to see the wonder of Redemption as secured for them in the Resurrection.

Surely this is the wonder of our faith. It gives us a new outlook. Let us become involved in the message of the Resurrection so that we too may share its gladness, not only with one another but with the world of men who stand this day in desperate need of its power and of its light.

THE LEGACY OF CHRIST

I am come that they might have life, and that they might
have it more abundantly. JOHN 10:10

One of the most interesting realities of life focuses on the numerous
benefits that have been given to us by others. The great benefactors
have been countless and they number men and women in every
age who have given much in their day for the amelioration of
human life and suffering. But not only that. In their deaths many
of them have provided well for the things that they loved while
they were alive. Many of the great social and religious institutions
of our world today actually live on through the gifts that have
come to them by way of endowments. Much of the work that is
being carried on today is actually being carried on by the labours,
the thoughtfulness and the generosity of those who no longer live
among us.

We rarely think of this but it is a fact that our whole existence,
from the cradle to the grave, is interwoven with others who have
opened up the paths and the doors through which we have passed.
We enjoy even now the fruits of their labour. While it is always
good for men and women to do all they can while they live to
make their mark upon our world of humanity, nevertheless we
should never forget that we can live on in our deeds and in our
gifts after we have passed from this mortal scene. The spiritual
and material legacies that we can pass on are many. Everyone
should endeavour to make such a contribution.

There was no one who ever came to our world with a more
beneficent heart, a more gracious mind and a more generous spirit
than Jesus. There was no one who touched life more than did
our Lord. No matter where He went somehow or another all knew
that He was present. This then is the Legacy of Christ.

Let us first look at what Jesus brought. He brought a new
conception of God to humanity. Whereas in the past God was
distant, now He was brought nearer by Jesus Christ. For the first
time men began to see that God was interested in their welfare
and loved them because man was part of His creation. For the
first time the old religions and their conceptions of God were
challenged. For the first time men began to see that these
unflinching truths about religion were not necessarily so. Their

minds and their hearts were, by the coming of Christ, now liberated.

This liberation that Jesus brought for humanity established a new sense of values. It came at a time when people were subjected to many restrictions. There was a tendency for people to get themselves all "hot and bothered" over directions they considered as absolutely necessary to their peace and happiness. Jesus would say, "Let us have men and women with right qualities, with a deep sense of values in any country, and secondary matters will eventually take care of themselves." He said, "Seek ye first the Kingdom of God and all these other things shall be added unto you." By bringing Himself to the world, Jesus brought God and when men looked at Him and heard Him speak they developed, for the first time, a new concept of God. Jesus made God what men needed to understand He was. Jesus called Him Father.

Let us look at what Jesus gave. Because He brought God and identified God with humanity, the new concept of the right action of men and women was born. For the first time they began to listen to the great words, "O, that my people would harken unto me then would they have peace like a river." Look at the rivers that have furnished great power and upon whose waters ships sail. As long as a river moves peacefully between its banks, it is a boon to humanity but let it get out of hand and it will tell its own story of devastation and destruction. Paul caught the sense of right actions when he wrote, "Whatsoever things are true, whatsoever things are honest, whatsoever things are just, whatsoever things are pure, whatsoever things are lovely, whatsoever things are of good report. If there be any virtue, if there be any praise, think on these things."

This great concept of right action brought about proper relationships between men and nations. In right relationships men become concerned with each other and with their needs and consequently there comes that feeling of putting some lasting principle at the centre of life. The centre of life is Jesus Christ Himself. The world needs nothing more at the centre, than our Lord.

What Jesus brought and what He gave are very important. However, our discussion would be incomplete without exploring the concept of what He left. He did not leave money or houses, or bonds or books. He was too poor for that. He said, "Foxes have holes and the birds of the air have nests but the Son of man has no place where to lay his head." Money and property are tangible assets but these are things that perish or pass away. Jesus left the unperishable things, the abiding things and when He returned to His Father He left a certain quality in which His disciples found newness of life. When they died it was still uncorrupted. Time has not changed what He has left nor have the years diminished His Gospel. All life is wrapped up in His great contention,

I am come that they might have life.

Why are we here? What have we brought to the world? What are we giving the world? What are we leaving the world? As disciples of Jesus Christ we are called upon to honour in our lives and in our labours, the mind and the spirit of our Master. Our Lord would never measure our life merely by what we have gotten out of it so much as what we have put into it. When we look at the Church of Christ today we are looking at Him. The Church is not rendering in His name, His purpose or doing His service until she learns to give to men a Saviour of the World, to bring a newness of heart and the life that He has to offer. The Church is called upon to put these qualities of the Master into practice. These qualities can be ours when we are ready to reconsecrate ourselves to His cause and to His Church and with clear thinking and with a spirit of dedication that makes us unafraid, go forward in His name to be men and women of God.

Things may not be as we want them but our faith can make them better than they are. Tennyson puts it this way,

She sees the best that glimmers through the worst,
She feels the sun is hid but for a night,
She spies the summer through the winter's bud,
She tastes the fruit before the blossom falls,
She hears the lark within the songless egg,
She finds the fountain where they wailed "Mirage".

If we are willing to do this we would be obeying Him who is the Lord of all life, the Saviour of all men.

NO OTHER GODS

Thou shalt have no other gods before Me. EXODUS 20:3

Modern man often wonders what such ancient words, addressed to a primitive and undisciplined people, have to do with us today. After all, Israel was a nation that worshipped idols. Their leaders were idolatrous and the people revelled in licentiousness. But it was because they were such a people that God gave them this commandment.

All this may sound very remote to us in the twentieth century. Few of us have seen an idol save in a museum. Our temptations are not the temptations of ancient people so we can without compunction dismiss this commandment as lacking relevance. Nonetheless, false belief in the first century or the twentieth century leads to wrong actions and idolatry is always the fruits of wrong actions.

It seems to be a popular pastime, for men of liberal thought, to discredit one's belief in God. They forget that a person's actions are always conditioned by a person's beliefs. The first commandment will outlive its critics and will endure every persecution. To men of all nations the word of God says, "Thou shalt have no other gods." We may feel we have advanced a long way from the shadow of Mount Sinai with its stern legations but Mount Sinai stands as one of the great judgment seats of history. Its laws were no mere conventions of an obscure nation. They were the revelations of the basic conditions of a man's being, that for that moment flamed into light that he might see his way and learn righteousness.

If man does not have right beliefs about God he is not right anywhere else in his life. There are some who are of the opinion that it doesn't really matter what a man believes. After all, belief is a private concern. That is a most dangerous lie!

Was it a private matter when German youth believed that the state was God and began to replace the religion of the Cross with the religion of race and blood? Was it a private matter when every young Japanese grew up in the belief that the Emperor was divine? Was it a private matter when Mussolini's belief in power caused his planes to destroy the helpless Ethiopians? Long before these people had broken the other commandments, "Thou shalt not steal"; "Thou shalt not kill", they had broken this first one, "Thou shalt have no other gods." When we stood in the ruined cities of Italy and Germany and looked at the devastation, we could not help but remember that here were nations where man thought he did not need God.

This commandment is not intended to be confined to a book. This commandment is for man's life — your life and mine. Today we, too, must be on our guard against the false gods that we worship.

One of these is the god of nationalism. Nationalism today sets itself up as an idol to be worshipped and brushes aside the God of Christianity. The god of nationalism, with its bloody terrorism, deprives man of his inalienable right to a belief in a living God. Hence, as believers, we are always in the business of rescuing our Christian heritage from the evil forces of our age. Our Christian interpretation of life needs to be stated amid the rival claimants of the day. We live by what is true and strong in us, not by what is false and weak. It is only faith in God and worship of God that can provide adequate protection against the dangers that menace us from without and from within. The only way that we can meet the scourge of this false paganism is by having a positive belief in the living and abiding God. Rabid nationalism is spreading like a cancer in our world today. It can only be destroyed when men restate and relive their faith in God. All men who hold this faith must be proclaimers of it and be ready at all times to stand firm in a common allegiance to serve the true God.

Racism is another false god that is gaining a great deal of support and it too is dangerous to the very being of any nation. We in Canada, are not exempt from this evil. There are people in our midst who are making much of their race, their colour and their creed. Daily we see to what depths man will go to satisfy this lust within his own heart. It is time now for men who hold such high and holy beliefs to make their presence felt and declare before our nation and the world that it is righteousness that exalteth the nation. This is the only way that we can eradicate man's inhumanity to man.

Many of us have forgotten that it is God who has made of one blood, all nations to dwell upon the face of the earth. This is a truth that needs to be declared; that needs to be honoured.

It also needs to be practiced. This is an evil that must be destroyed and it can only be destroyed when we harken to the words of the commandment, "Thou shalt have no other gods." This is surely the message that men and nations must hear, heed and exercise with a passion that will breakdown walls that separate man from man and nation from nation. We must bring to bear our belief upon the folly of man's own heart.

Then, too, there is the god of selfishness, or self-indulgence, that is being worshipped today. The desire for personal and selective security has blinded our eyes to the needs of others. When this happens our belly becomes our god, our passions become our evils and we lose ourselves in the desire to feed upon that which cannot last and that which does not satisfy the human heart. Discerning minds have seen the insanity of the world becoming more chronic. We burn food while people starve! Factories are crammed with garments while the poor lack the protection from bitter winds! Where is the sanity here?

There is only one way that we can meet and destroy these false gods that come to our lives and leave them in ruin. These false gods that blatantly destroy the soul of man and weaken his character. These false gods that demand a high price for our worship. Jesus, our Lord, gives us the answer,

> Love the Lord, your God, with all your mind
> and with all your strength,
> remembering that you cannot serve two masters.

Have firm convictions and you will have no problem with the reality of God, the trustworthiness of Jesus, the efficacy of prayer, the duty of service and the kinship of men. Be fixed, I beseech you on the things that are fixed by a Sovereign God. Hold fast the centralities of the faith. Always remember that the Gospel is not the invention of last week. It is the message once delivered to the saints and for two thousand years men have sailed by its dependable chart. Many a storm has beaten upon it. There have been dark ages in which only the few have taken its counsel while the multitude have passed it by. Still it serves.

Those who travel in the convoy that employs this chart need not fear the multiplying perils of the day. They will not travel alone and will come safely to their journey's end. John Wesley sums it up for all of us in one of his great hymns,

Fixed on this ground will I remain,
Though my heart fail and flesh decay.
This anchor shall my soul sustain,
When earth's foundations melt away.
Mercy's full power I then shall prove
Loved with an everlasting love.

This is not easy ground upon which to stand when false gods are seeking to gain our friendship and allegiance. Still, if what we have been trying to say is true, let us remember that the least noticed member of society makes his or her contribution to the intellectual, moral and spiritual atmosphere when in league with God. Let us therefore as men and women who have declared our faith and our belief in God, who have been influenced by His power, who know the meaning of His presence, go out and sweeten by our faith the atmosphere of the home, our country and the world. There are times when all the things that we have loved and cherished seem under the sentence of death. But not for naught have you lived and reflected the light of heaven. God will still vindicate His own.

Easter follows Good Friday. The night is dark, but thank God, joy cometh in the morning.

JUSTIFICATION BY FAITH

Therefore being justified by faith, we have peace with
God through our Lord Jesus Christ. ROMANS 5:1

We come this evening to consider one of the most important steps on our way to God. It will be necessary as it was for Paul to clear the path and seek to show that the way to God is not found in the formal customs of religion or in the acts of worship. These by themselves have no value and are to be considered secondary in importance when the soul is seeking direct access to God. Paul in this letter is attacking a rigid formula that demanded an exact outward form of religion to an inner and personal relationship with God. He himself had been a slave to the law and a careful observer of all that it demanded. He had experienced in his own heart the great life that comes to one who is lifted by God to a place of rich, personal surety through faith in Christ. So he continues to give expression to a faith that demands the complete commitment of the heart to God, for only in this way can the needed peace between God and man be achieved.

From this text we are to learn how such an important experience is to be achieved. Many centuries have passed since these words were spoken and as we review the onward march of the Church, we see at times how she has drifted from this all important religious experience. Where the Church or the individual drifts from personal contact with God, the natural result is corruption and spiritual poverty.

It was this doctrine that gave birth to the Reformation in Germany. Luther stated that it was this doctrine that distinguished a standing or falling Church. Luther was the son of God-fearing parents and was brought up from his youth to live a religious life. He had always the fear of God before him. In the presence of death he was driven to a more earnest striving after God. He took refuge in a monastery and was afterwards ordained as a priest. It was commonly believed that by doing good works which included penances and gifts to the Church of money and service, a man could merit salvation. It was on the holy staircase in Rome while performing prayers in an effort to obtain indulgences, that the great truth, "The just shall live by faith", came home to Luther's heart. He rose and left the place. This experience was to him the beginning of a new life. He had entered into a personal relationship with Jesus Christ.

The tendency today is to drift from faith's principles to rely on human principles. Inevitably this will have a negative religious effect upon the Church. There needs to be a re-echoing of the fundamental principles of our faith. I believe that justification by faith is the very essence of the Gospel message, and anything that is seeking to stand between the soul and God must be met in the same challenging manner as was demonstrated by Paul, Luther and many other great leaders of the Reformed Church.

In the first place, what is it that comes between a man and God? Clearly, it is the consciousness of our sins. I realize that this is the very thing that we don't want to hear about. This is a subject that we'd rather not discuss. It is, by its very nature, the thing that we would seek to hide and gloss over. We will do almost anything to escape its indictment. The result is that we find human effort being put forth to meet the needs of the human heart.

In the Roman Catholic Church men confess their sins to a priest; Buddhism, with its painstaking human efforts, seeks, by a denial of life itself, to relieve the soul of sin; Hinduism, with its philosophy of life, is seeking to overcome sin by attributing to man divinity achieved through knowledge.

One could go on to summarize how the religions of the world are seeking to deal with the problem of sin. Enough has been said to remind us that many the world over are seeking to settle the matter on human grounds. This cannot be done. The hardest place to confront men with sin is in the Church. It is the place where many of us feel we are free from sin. We are confronting the same problem in the Church today that the Reformers fought against and indeed gave their lives for. We need to know afresh that the way to God is through personal faith in Jesus Christ. Only through such an experience can man be justified.

I want to warn you against the many substitutes being offered today to obtain the peace of God. Take, for example, the "hereditary religious affiliation" dogma that many are putting forward to explain their religious experience. I asked a man the other day about his Christian life and how it came about that he found himself in the Church. He told me that his father and mother were Presbyterians and that he was brought up a Presbyterian, hereby explaining his Christian inclinations. Man is not justified by nominal attachment to a Church but by an actual relationship to Jesus Christ. It is not what God has done for our parents but what He has done for us, by a personal faith in Him, that justifies us in His holy presence. It is having the sin in our own hearts put to rest that brings us to a communion with God.

There are those who are seeking justification through the exercise of morality. They count their goodness as a requirement for religious experience. They may rigidly observe an ethical code. They may be pure, just, truthful, lovable and with all that not be numbered with the Redeemed. They may, in fact, show themselves to be the worst kind of enemy to Christianity, as the apostle was before he was humbled on the road to Damascus. Morality is but one of the chief aims of a Christian life but it must not be interpreted as that which can justify a man in the sight of God.

Charity is another substitute that is used today to purchase the indulgence of heaven. Many are trying to buy their way to God. They feel if they are giving a hundred cents to the dollar and making generous gifts to the work of the Lord, that in some way they will be justified. It is true that generosity is one of the virtues of Christianity but it is never prompted by ulterior motives. There are many who are ready to part with their money before they are ready to part with their lives and dedicate them to God. Charity may ease a troubled conscience but it cannot purchase the justification of God.

Justification is not the acceptance of a definite creed. It is here that so much of our religious life is nothing more, in the eyes of God, than the worst kind of hypocrisy. It is very easy to get men and women to give assent to creeds and rituals that have been formulated by the Church but it is very hard to get them to give positive allegiance to the person behind the creed. Here, I believe that we can explain the cause of so much dissatisfaction within the Church today. There are many today who think that because they have accepted the creeds of the Church they are entitled to be reckoned with the saved, even though they have still to make a personal surrender of their lives to Christ. They are trying to find satisfaction for their souls through a human relationship with the Church, instead of a Divine relationship with Christ.

Against such false notions must we stand. We must assert that justification cannot be achieved or experienced through human acts, such as penance, discipline, morality, generosity or the acceptance of creeds. It can only be experienced when through a deep sense of sin, we seek through a personal faith in Christ, a removal of our sin.

Come home then to God. He will receive you and sanctify your life. He will tell you that in His heart your place has never been lost. He has been waiting to tell you that sin is your worst enemy and because of it you have been a long way from home and a long time out of His love and righteousness. It is true that we can only come with imperfect penitence and faltering faith, but we must come confessing that there are many reasons why He should reject us. There is only one reason why He should receive us, that our sin has been atoned for by His own infinite love. This coming to God, unworthy though we be, is exercising what could be described as the doctrine of justification by faith.

We need this direct association with God and it is only in such a fellowship that we can be the men and women that God can use for His honour and the advancement of His Kingdom among men. Have you this personal assurance of God? Have you this personal faith which He offers? If not, your place is to come to the mercy seat today, acknowledging that you are a sinner in need of a Saviour. He is waiting for you. He is ready to bid you welcome into His great and matchless love. Life is too short to live it apart from God and the life that comes from God is the life that each and every one of us need.

THE CHRISTIAN HOME

Except the Lord build the house, they labour in vain that build it.
PSALM 127:1

The oldest and most influential institution in our society is the home. While it has undergone many physical changes, its function remains the same. The preservation of the home is imperative for without it the moral and spiritual influence of the nation will be threatened. The home today is being tested by social and economic changes, changes indeed that have not always been in its best interest. Some homes have been able to stand bravely; other have succumbed. The welfare of children is still the major responsibility of parents. It is not a responsibility to be transferred to any agency, whether such an agency be the school, the Church or any other organization.

Parents today have a real task on their hands. It is not easy to raise children in a modern society. Our sons and daughters are children of the twentieth century and their lives must be lived and molded in the day and hour in which they exist. The opportunities today are by and large much greater, but preparation for life is more demanding and more exacting than has been the lot of any other generation. My plea today is not so much for the moral assessment of our sons and daughters but for a reassessment of our privileged positions as parents. In the majority of cases, children in attitude and conduct are but a reflection of their parents. We determine in the long run what the final destination of our children will be. Remember you still get good trees from good seed!

Our text suggests first of all, that the foundation of the home must be laid by the Lord. A most challenging issue. All authority and obedience when vested in the Lord assures the home of the foundation that is necessary for its life and for its welfare. Someone has said, "Be sure of the foundation and the superstructure will take care of itself." Fathers and mothers of the twentieth century need to be warned that unless they exercise in love, authority and obedience, they will be in real difficulty. We cannot afford to transfer or surrender our responsibility. If we do, we will eventually lose both the control and the respect of our children. Rebellion is a natural thing, yet as parents we have the right to require, through love, obedience.

Obedience and authority in the home are necessary. It has been demonstrated that it is best shared by parents who together, with mutual consent and understanding, provide their children with this ingredient, so necessary to formulate character. I know that this is a high ideal but without it we are apt to go astray. No nation has ever made any progress in a downward direction. No people have ever become great by lowering their standards. It is not progress if the moral tone is lower than it was. It is not progress when purity is not as sweet as it used to be. It is not progress when parenthood loses it fragrance. Whatever else it is, it is not progress and our children suffer.

Authority and obedience are necessary ingredients to hold the frame together. It is only in this way that direction can be given to our children. When we have set the foundation of the home in a common and mutual faith in God, then as parents our aim and purpose for our children becomes clearer. I know that our generation is witnessing changes in the structure of the home emerging from the bewildering confusion of our times. We, in Canada, have a higher standard of living than any other country or at any other time in the history of the world. We have more automobiles, more movies, more telephones, more money, more radios, more televisions, more night clubs, more crime, more divorce, than any other nation our size.

As parents, I know that we want our children to enjoy the advantages of the day. We want our children to get a good education. Certainly, we want our children to succeed. The aim and the purpose is to make our homes Christian, to give our children some religious moorings rather than some vague kind of idealism espoused in some popular modern novel.

The best results can be achieved from our children when the home and the Church find a common denominator. The Church stands today as a great teacher of the principles of Christ and without this kind of Christian education, without these principles of Christ at work, we are in danger of raising our children as pagans.

Observe the hymn, "When mothers of Salem their children brought to Jesus". There is a truth here that needs to be stressed. They didn't send their children, they didn't entrust them to the care of someone else. These mothers of Salem were wise. They brought their children to Jesus. This is one of the things that as parents we must learn to do today. If you never enter a Church it is rather futile to send your child to Sunday School. Our homes need the fresh and vital experience of God. When that is present then we can pass on to our children some of the great and worthy things to make them strong. I see enough every day to know that many parents are neglecting this responsibility. When it is neglected, then we lose the very anchor that will hold us sure and steadfast against the great storms that battle us in life.

I am appealing for the Christian home, for the presence of Christ in our homes, for the lifting of the shade so that His light can shine into our hearts and we can pass on to our children a heritage untarnished — a heritage that will give our children a foundation upon which to build a greater and better life.

THE BLESSED NAME OF MOTHER

Some words gather meaning as they journey until at last they overflow and become symbols of things too deep for speech. The word "mother", just like the words "home" and "country", did not mean much when first uttered. It was simply used as a term of distinction and carried with it no special significance.

But it has been redeemed and now stands for everything that is sacred, holy and sublime.

Every day ought to be Mother's Day. Never a sun should set until we have paid worthy tribute to that immortal host who has replenished and blessed the earth. Whatever excuse other ages may have had for being blind to the glory of motherhood, there is no plausible pretext for such indifference today. The progress of the centuries makes such an attitude impossible. With all our deepened insight and quickened sense of appreciation, there have come to us conceptions of motherhood that evoke reverence, merit worship and leave us with a multitude of hallowed memories. We cannot help but join hands and hearts with those who are praising God for the noble women who have enriched and enraptured life.

Motherhood is the highest privilege of womanhood. There is no limit to its kingdom and its influence never dies. God has wreathed it with the crown immortal and decked it with the fairest flowers that come from His gracious hand. Whatever other gifts and powers may gleam and glow in the halls of history, the creative spirit of motherhood is the brightest and most benevolent of all. There is a price to pay for such an honour. Royal favours never come in common colours. The great things wear a scarlet border. A mother has a pain to bear for every joy she carries, but what does suffering avail when the blood-stained Cross becomes her glory and proves a lasting blessing to the world.

I want to trace the grandeur of that spirit. It has meant so much to us that we cannot ignore it. There are none among us who have not said of their mother,

> Because you love me I have found
> New joys that were not mine before;
> New stars have lighted up my sky
> With glories growing more and more.
>
> Because you love me, I can rise.
> To the heights of fame and realms of power;
> Because you love me, I may learn
> The highest use of every hour.

These attainments have been embodied in our mother's dreams. It fills the cup of joy when little children come into our home. Their very presence is the fulfillment of long cherished hopes and yet when they come and prattle at our feet, the mother has started to dream anew. The outlook of the matron and maid are vastly different.

The mother keeps the immediate happiness of self in the background and spends her days dreaming of her children's future. She cannot draw the little ones to her breast nor watch them at play in the nursery, or listen to their childish babblings, but she sees away into the coming days. In every scene she pictures only what is worthiest and best for those who are her own. She desires her children to be healthy in body and strong in mind. She craves to see them comfortably settled in some business or profession. She wants to see them enjoy a high and honourable place among men, make the most of their talents and render a royal service to the community and the nation. The very thought of the consummation of her visions makes her bosom swell with pride.

But alas the days of dreaming for the young mother are sometimes the happiest days she will ever know. There are ghosts that come and touch our hand and things that happen to spoil our best plans. Life on earth ofttime mingles joy with sorrow. Children have barely blessed our home when hideous thoughts arise. What if something should intervene and take our little one away? Where could we find happiness then? These thoughts speak with a fuller accent whenever the little folk we so dearly love become ill.

But as the years advance, there are other fears that haunt the mother. There are things that steal across her imagination to torture a thousand times over: social dishonour, moral debasement, spiritual poverty, eternal ruin. She covets the best for her children and nothing less than the best can satisfy her heart. Who among us will dare to wound her spirit and send the swordpoint through her loving soul! If we could only be made to realize how she prays for us and how she follows us everywhere we go with yearnings for our safety, prosperity and peace.

Mothers have scores of intricate problems to solve. The proper support and education of her family must be attended to, but these are by no means the deepest perplexities. It is not long before she notices that her children are not all alike. The difference in temperament early asserts itself. One child will have sweet and winsome ways and another will be rough and boisterous. One will be obedient and find the greatest delight at home and still another will be rebellious and find more joy among comparative strangers. One will have religious inclinations and another seems determined to drift with the world.

As the years roll on, the mother is beset with more difficulties. Sometimes children cease to share their secrets. Sometimes they try to hide their plans and make it clearly understood that they want no meddling. Sometimes they resent interference about personal habits and the choice of companions. They reach that stage when they deem themselves wholly independent. They imagine that they are full grown while yet in their teens. When the mother ventures to offer suggestions and counsel the children, they sometimes scoff as though she were utterly ignorant of the demands of life and in her ideals, a generation behind the times.

I tell you it takes a mother to have a tireless patience, a dauntless faith and a boundless love if she would win her children to the right and make them know that she is by far the best friend that they have. It takes her to resort continually to the throne of grace, if she would find strength for her arduous tasks and the needed light for the darkened way.

A mother, of course, has her peculiar temptations. There are seasons when she becomes thoroughly discouraged. The tide and storm seem to be against her and every earnest effort appears to be in vain. Her holiest visions have not been realized. Her fondest hopes have not come true. It appears as if all her love and faithfulness and every endeavour has been wasted. Sometimes in the cold grip of that sense of failure the mother is tempted to give up in hopeless despair. What is the use of all this devotion if the children make a jest of it? Why teach them to pray when they make a mockery of religion and go out and deliberately do what's wrong? How could they expect us to care for them if they have no consideration for us? Is there any possible advantage in denying ourselves when our sacrifices are treated so lightly?

There are many mothers who have reasoned things out just in that way. It is little wonder when we consider the wanton indifference which so boldly asserts itself among so many of our young men and women. To every crestfallen mother I would say this: Never give up! It is wiser and better always to hope than to dance to despair!

There are times when it is hard for the mother to accept that counsel and no time more so, perhaps, then when she is left strangely alone. Sometimes God Himself takes her little one away and bereft of her treasure she weeps in the lonely shadows. Sometimes her children go off to settle on distant shores. She watches in vain for the overdue letter. Sometimes her children get married and forget all about the loving hearts in the old homestead. Sometimes her sons and daughters who stay around the scenes of their childhood virtually forsake the one who gave them birth and reared them to manhood and womanhood. They have no time for fellowship with their mother. They never try to lighten her load of care. They never think that she needs the rest of recreation. They never dream of taking her out for a walk, and if they meet her on the street they pass her by with a careless nod. They live for self. They must have their fling and enjoy their pleasures. They must wear the best clothes and feast at the best tables. They must keep late hours and squander their time and money. And all the while for them their mothers are toiling, planning, worrying, sacrificing, hoping and praying.

I thank God that this is not always true and I want to say in His holy name that it should never be true. There are children who do their duty nobly. They show themselves to be true sons and daughters and true companions in the home. They have always a kindly smile, a cheery word, a feeling heart and a helping hand for mother. And if our thoughts can be translated into words you would hear something like this:

Who fed me from her gentle breast
And hushed me in her arms to rest,
And on my cheeks sweet kisses pressed?
My mother.

When pain and sickness made me cry
Who gazed upon my heavy eye,
And wept for fear that I should die?
My mother.

Who taught my infant lips to pray
To love God's holy word and day,
And walk in wisdom's pleasant way?
My mother.

And can I ever cease to be
Affectionate and kind to thee,
Who was so very kind to me -
My mother.

Oh, no, the thought I cannot bear
And if God please my life to spare,
I hope I shall reward thy care.
My mother.

THE ROAD TO FOLLOW

And an highway shall be there, and a way, and it shall be called
The way of holiness . . . the wayfaring men though fools,
shall not err therein. ISAIAH 35:8

A young man found himself at a job that required patience, diligence, competence and regularity. It was demanding and sometimes frustrating. One day he called upon his boss and told him that he wished to quit. "Quit", said the boss. "If you want to master it you stay with it."

This is good advice to the Christian and to all who are seeking to mold their lives according to the way of righteousness. Very often we are told that Christianity is too mysterious, too complex, too exacting to be accepted. Many people feel that they cannot be Christian because they fail to understand its meaning. It is quite true that Christianity was never intended to be an easy religion. It has it joys and its sorrows, its gains and its losses, its ups and its downs.

Since Christianity must dwell in imperfect humanity, much of our imperfectness is sometimes carried over into our religion.

The prophet instructs us that the way of holiness is a way which is demanding and sacrificial. Jesus Himself said, "Straight is the gate and narrow is the way." All this is found in the Christian faith.

I know that there are many fields of human endeavour where we forever remain as spectators. The field of medicine, for example, is one of them. Most of us do not understand medical terminology or medical diagnosis. Not long ago I remember listening to two astronomers discussing a formula calculated to work out the distance from one heavenly body to the other. I need hardly tell you that I was totally in the dark. They were speaking a language I did not comprehend. What I do know is that there is nothing quite so wonderful or beautiful as a starry night. I can appreciate that although I am ignorant of the astronomer's jargon.

There are many fields of human endeavour from which we are completely excluded simply because we are neither trained to understand nor are we in a position to appreciate the values attached to them. Be that as it may, the prophet goes on to assure us that there is one field in which no one is excluded, and his comforting words should help us as we worship, "and an highway shall be there, and a way, and it shall be called The way of holiness . . . the wayfaring men though fools, shall not err therein."

Although not a scholar or a theologian, you can travel the King's highway. No one denies the value of scholarship and the debt we owe to its toil, but I am speaking here of essential religion that can be proclaimed on a street corner or in a cathedral and can be grasped by those who can neither read nor write. The Gospel of Christ is so adapted to the human heart that an untutored man can grasp it. If man in other areas of human toil and exploration shut you out by his superior intelligence, remember, Christ takes you in and that is all that matters. The seed sown in the soil by a child will grow just as well as the seed sown by the hand of an expert. You do not have to be a learned theologian to be a Christian, all you need to do is to turn your face and your heart to Christ.

During the dark days of war most of our religion was condensed into a few essentials. A few simple truths: God is our Father; Jesus brings us to Him; a prayer is a real thing; guidance comes when you want to do right; death is not the end. Let the scholars do their work and we will honour it. If you know it all the better. If you don't you will be none the worse. As long as you know Christ as your personal Saviour you are on the right road, you are on the way of holiness and you will not err when you are on that road.

There is a way of holiness for you even though your days are full of "rush and fuss". Although you are busy people, tied down with the labours of the day, you have to work to keep your soul and body together and to meet the requirements of your family. That is what God wants all of us to do. The saint needs seclusion but you haven't time for that. Remember the mark of sainthood is character and you can have that whether you work in a mill or say your beads in a monastery. All saints do not wear clerical garb or are they venerated by their church. There are many saints today working in offices, homes, warehouses. There are parents everywhere today who, by their lives, are seeking to direct their children in the way of righteousness, who are permitting their children to grow in the faith by introducing them to the things of God.

Even though you feel there is much wrong today with the Church, please remember that if the Church is to live and be a force for good it requires your common touch and your simple faith. I know that the Church and its ministers have made it, at times, difficult for you to believe. We have strangled the revelation of Jesus by our creeds, our courts and our governments. We have retarded Christian progress because our own wishes have gotten in the way of Christ. As one dear elder said to a minister who was preaching for a call, "If you please me, you have a good chance of getting this pulpit." Maybe we have tried to please men and not Christ.

As Christian people we sometimes look in the wrong places and to the wrong things to advance the cause of righteousness. It is the duty of the Church to lead in all matters of righteousness, in civil, social and political life and seek to bring the Christian faith to bear upon the lives of men and women no matter what their vocation be.

Sometimes we have remained silent; sometimes we swing our hammers and flatten out some small abuse while cruel evils are allowed to attack the heart of our people and our nation. In spite of the wrong that may be evident and the silence that you may observe in your church, cultured or uncultured man, saint or sinner, the way of holiness is for you. But it is you, and only you, who can mend the wrongs. Not even a dumb and failing Church can alter your need of a Saviour. The road for you to follow is the road along which the Master leads. Your duty is plain. There is still a star to guide the humble. Trust in God and do the right.

I do not know the burden of your life today. Only God knows and that is just as well. But I do want you to feel that He is here to mend the broken cisterns of your life so that the waters of His righteousness may flow freely. Some of you may be like the young man. Because life has become too complex, too demanding, too burdensome, you want to quit, you want to give up. "If you want to master it, you stay with it." Remember how the Lord put it, "I am the way, the truth and the life."

If we make Christ central in our life, then we shall be able to meet the difficulties. Do not think for a moment that Christianity will allow you to avoid these things. What it does do, is provide the strength to bear the burden and the heat of the day.

Come forward bravely, believing that Jesus has a ministry for your life today. Freshen your faith in prayer and in meditation. Lift up your eyes unto the hills from whence cometh your help. This is the safe road to follow.

OVERCOMING EVIL

Deliver us from evil. LUKE 11:4

Most people would agree that we must get the best of evil and not allow it to get the best of us. Evil is the common enemy. The Master Himself put this prayer on our lips, "Deliver us from evil." The main question before us has to do with the method. How can we best overcome evil?

Some would tell us to leave it alone until by its own stupidity it perishes. We are not to fight vice and crime, injustice and greed. We are to bear with them patiently until some day they finally disappear. The policy of nonresistance has been advocated by some very fine people. They believe that the only passage in the

New Testament to be taken literally is, "Resist not evil". If a man smites you on the cheek, turn to him the other. If he compels you to go a mile, go two. If he takes away your coat, hand him your cloak also. In other words, speak softly and do not go around carrying a big stick!

These words of counsel may have had a certain value for a particular situation. It is by no means clear that they were ever intended to furnish us with a universal and permanent program of action. That is not the way to get rid of the black plague, the yellow fever or smallpox. It is not the method that is being used to get rid of malaria, typhoid fever, tuberculosis and cancer. We do not sit down in the presence of those enemies of human wellbeing and fold our hands saying, "Resist not evil". In all the ways that medical science and wise sanitation can devise, we are fighting them to the limit. We are fighting ignorance and super-stition and inefficiency with a well-organized and well-supported public school system. We are lining up for a more resolute attack on poverty and poor housing, upon the evils of unemployment and the disability of old age. We believe these social evils can be cured but the cure will not come by simply letting them alone. They are to be fought from the rising of the sun until the stars appear.

First of all let us look at our backgrounds. Our days are filled with trial. With all the nations of the world in a tizzy, it is difficult to stand up for right action. It is not easy to stand for the things that are Christian in the home, in business, in politics, in recreation and education. The Master warned us in advance that it would not be easy, "In this world ye will have tribulation but be of good cheer. I have overcome."

We are confronted on every side with problems and perils that we cannot see through or around. We have problems of intemperance, greed, social snobbery, delinquency, racial preju-dice, indifference to God in His Church. The evils are many. Enough indeed that they crucify our Lord afresh every day. Is there anything we can do about it? Is there anything as a Christian Church that we can do to stem the tide and turn the flow into the rich service of Jesus Christ? Are we just going to sit down and fold our hands. As long as I am safe what need I care?

Somehow we cannot turn away and seek some safe refuge

for there are simply no safe places any more. Evil lurks on every corner and has a friend in every roadway. Brute force and cruelty are the order of the day. The end, they say, justifies the means.

Our weapons must be carefully chosen. They certainly must not be weapons of the carnal. They must be spiritual. We are here to put on the whole armour of God, that we might be able together as Christians, to stand fast and see the ugly business of evil wiped from the surface of the world. We need to believe that the Lord of Hosts is with us. The God of Jacob is our refuge. It is His battle more than it is ours. We are honour bound as Christians to follow His methods. Remember He must reign until He has put all enemies under His feet. He is not our Lord unless He can honour His claims and honour them He will. The fortress of the Christian is the everlasting arms of Christ, our King and Lord.

There are many attitudes confronting us in society today. People stand up and exclaim that God is good, God is all, all is good and there is no such thing as sin, pain, disease or death. The facts are against them. People with their feet on the ground and with heads on their shoulders know better. They have the evidence of their senses. Christ recognized the presence of evil and suffering in this world of ours. He said, "The kingdom of heaven is like a man who soweth good seed in his field and while men slept under cover of darkness his enemy came and sowed tares among the wheat. When the wheat sprung up so also did the tares."

Turn it and twist it as we may, life is a battle against hostile forces. All our harvests have to be reaped in fields where weeds grow. All of our gains have to be secured in the very teeth of opposition.

I am not suggesting that we have the answer to all these problems nor do I always know why people suffer. I do think, however, that we will know how to work against evil if we use the method that Jesus has demonstrated. We need to know first of all, that the enemy is here in full force. But we are called to maintain the position of righteousness believing that, in its power we can meet, we can overcome and we can destroy evil.

If our position as Christian people in the world today appears to be precarious, it is only so because we have stopped believing that God is the Wise Orderer of all that is good and wholesome for His children. Always remember that the righteousness of Christ is never conditioned by the righteousness of the world. Rather, is the world conditioned by the laws of righteousness vested in Jesus Christ.

If the enemy is here in full force then we must assert ourselves in our faith, to meet the conflict. We must be brave in showing our faith and using our gifts to dispel the darkness, to rout the enemy again and again and prepare ourselves for new conflicts. If we lose one fight — a little skirmish here, a little skirmish there — we tend to throw up our hands in despair. That is not the way that the Kingdom of Righteousness is to be built, nor is that the way the enemy can be defeated. The compromising spirit, the middle way from which we all suffer, is not the answer. Sin can never produce good, so consequently we are out there showing to the world that it is the righteousness of God that brings goodness and hope to the lives of men. I know that this can never be an easy or a popular position to maintain. Nonetheless, it is the only position that we can maintain and the only position that we can really accept.

Our business, as Christians, is to raise wheat and not particularly to destroy weeds. We become quite negative in our Christian life. We go around denouncing and showing our disrespect for those who are not on our side. We are too ready to brand people. Too ready to tag them. And so it is that the great cause that confronts us all in this land and every land, is to realize that there must be more cultivation of the Christian spirit. There must be more sowing of the seed of righteousness. Let us prepare ourselves for that type of labour and when we put some effort into it then we will realize that it is more important to be giving ourselves to the raising of wheat, to the raising of men and women, in the name of Christ.

We do more for the Kingdom of God by winning men than denouncing them. It requires patience to do this kind of work. Patience does not mean complacency. It does not mean that we sit idly by. It means, as it meant for the man who built his house on a rock, to do some sensible planning so that when the storm comes the house is able to resist the tempest.

If we are going to understand our Christian faith, it requires patience. It takes patience to learn to pray. It takes patience to read the Word of God. It requires patience to do any kind of Christian work. Unless we can gather this patience and make it part and parcel of our character then it is hardly likely that we will become other than fair weather Christians. When Jesus delivered men from evil He released them for the cause of good. This is precisely what happens in the Christian faith. Evil is always overcome by good. In His name I ask you to accept this thought and this truth for your soul's welfare today.

RESTORING THE FAITH

So build we the wall; — for the people had a mind to work.
NEHEMIAH 4:6

Since the prophet is a man who always speaks for God, he is always coming into conflict with the moral conditions of the world. Nehemiah did much more than merely rebuild the walls of Jerusalem. He knew in his own heart where the true strength of Zion lay — her essential foundations, her true progress, her eternal greatness. Surrounding all this was her spiritual understanding of God. If these foundations be removed, all would fall apart. What the prophet attempted to do was to activate by his zeal, a fresh faith in God and bring this understanding of God to bear upon the life and the work of the children of Israel. His reformation could never accomplish anything unless it had these elements of daring in it. He knew in his own heart that in order to restore he must reform.

Since the religious, political and social conditions of the day have their counterpart in our own, I desire to meet with you on the same ground to see to what degree our spiritual advance is being retarded. Has our faith any consolation? Has it any true merit to meet the forces of evil that attack us? Have we in our lives to restore some broken walls that have fallen because of our carelessness or our personal neglect?

The first great issue facing the Church today is the issue of the Bible and the Reformation. Here, like Nehemiah, we must be brave enough to begin at the centre and not at the circumference. It could be that by apathy we have allowed ourselves to be exposed to every enemy and every danger. We have permitted the strong defences of our faith to crumble and fall down. We have gone about preaching that it does not matter what a man believes so long as he is a good fellow and a decent citizen. We have forsaken our Christian obligations and our duties. We have left to flounder, the permanent things — the things that have meant most in our lives and in our day.

Somehow, we have permitted ourselves to interpret our Christian freedom as a right to absent ourselves from the House of God and thus deprive ourselves of a sense of God. In doing this we forget our religious obligations. Too long we have listened to questions concerning the integrity of men who challenge us with Christian truth. We are past masters at hiding in smug complacency. The enemy who stands outside the citadel of our being is content to win his battle for sin without a fight and silently advance his vicious struggle for our lives and for our ideals. We fall into the trap of allowing newspapers, novels, periodicals, radio and television to do our thinking. We have forgotten the sole authority that is ours, that is the Word of God. We have forgotten that God's word is our guide in all spiritual matters and in the maintenance of moral integrity.

Perhaps the Church has become a quiet flowing river carrying deadwood rather than a surging stream whose purpose is to generate power and vitality. Israel's tragedy is our own. In light she wandered from God and in light she discarded her religious rights. Like Nehemiah we must be brave enough to see our sin and courageous enough to do something about it. If our faith is to be reformed and revived we must have cleansing from within. Our spiritual poverty must be met by individual spiritual incentives and in these incentives we must discover first of all that God is our God, a personal God.

We must learn to believe that man's chief end is to glorify God and to enjoy Him forever. Are we sure we have this spiritual incentive? Have we given our lives over to this spiritual contention? There can be no revival or rebuilding of the faith until we have settled our relationship and our responsibility to the living and the abiding Christ. We are faced with two alternatives: either we disregard the requirements of Christ and continue to live in sin, which in a sense is indifference, or we make a clean breast of our weariness, our wandering and our striving before Him and in mercy seek His forgiveness and His guidance.

Having established that we care for God and love Christ, we enter into the business of doing the work of God. Every man, in God's name, on the job for Him. The trowel and the sword is the line of advance. Certainly you will disturb the enemy. Please remember that evil has nothing to fear from a do-nothing faith or a do-nothing Church. Let this faith awaken and declare itself and you will discover the forces of evil will be pitted against you.

We talk a great deal about the accomplishments that have been made in our world in the field of science, labour, social service and government. We all are indebted to those who have made their contribution in these fields. However, the time surely has come when the Church must declare its determination to make similar advances for the cause of Christ and for His Kingdom.

What then are the walls that we as a church must re-erect for the common good? First of all, it would suggest that there must be a deeper interest in Christian worship. I am referring here to worship devoid of sentiment or of those things that purport only a showy substance of our faith. I am referring here to worship that brings a total dependence upon God where we continually set our minds and hearts in His direction. Worship that will cleanse us, keep us free from sin and make us glad that we have spent our days and our hours in the House of God. Through worship we will be able to see our place in the Church and out of this will grow a desire to advance the purity of worship in our life and a willingness to be all out and all in, for the cause of God in our lives. Linked with worship there is the sense of reverence and in reverence we discover the power and person of God in our lives. The glitter and colour of the world is lost in our understanding of being a child of God, an adherent of His love, a creature of His care.

Quite naturally out of worship and reverence, there comes a new attachment to God in our lives. This attachment links us directly with the work that must be ours as disciples of Jesus Christ. A man cannot have a divided loyalty. Loyalty to one's faith involves one in the cause of one's faith. As a church we must meet every challenge that would belittle the dignity of God in human life. We must learn afresh the value of the redeeming power of Christ in human life.

Rebuilding these walls will put a strain on our faith, which of necessity is essential. We are all too prone today to be a little careless and listless in the faith. The time has come when Christ is calling us to new service. This is the day that we must give ourselves completely to Him. These are the walls that we must rebuild in His name.

WHY GO TO CHURCH?

Give unto the Lord the glory due unto His name: bring an offering, and come into His courts. PSALM 96:8

It is the duty of every Christian man and woman to go to church. Duty is something that is due and which we are bound to pay. One must pay one's debts to others and surely our debt to God must not be regarded more lightly than our debts to each other.

Worship is due. God expects it. God asks us to praise Him, but He asks and requires us to do this for our own sake not His. We can add nothing to His greatness and majesty. He knows that only by lifting up our hearts to Him, by thinking of the beauty, truth and purity that are in Him, can we as men and women attain the real dignity of our creation. Worship, then, is our debt to God, and we must pay our debt. Show me a man who does his duty because it is his duty, and not for what he may get by doing it, and there you will find a man who is not far from the Kingdom of God.

But we worship not only because it is our duty, but because it is our delight. Worship is a thing that we are glad and eager to do and nothing will hinder us from doing it. This is the only true spirit of worship. The worship of the man who is glad when it is said to him, "Let us go up into the house of the Lord." We give honour to whom honour is due among men. Why do so many who are ever so anxious to perform such honour, refuse to render it to God, which surely they must admit belongs to Him. They will salute their country's flag and show loyal respect to the Queen. They willingly render to Caesar the things that are Caesar's. Why then so reluctant are they to render to God the things that are God's?

We go to church to witness to the Resurrection of Christ. Every Lord's Day we enter into His house, we are once more pledging our faith anew to Him and thanking Him for what He did in His Resurrection for all mankind. There are many reasons put forth by people for going to church or not going to church: "Our minister is a fine preacher." "I like to go now and then when the minister has a special sermon." "That new man of ours cannot preach like the old man so I have stopped going." "I can't stick that choir." "That church of ours is too cold. I catch cold everytime I go", pleads some robust looking man who will stand in line in the dead of winter waiting to get tickets to a hockey game. "I would go if the minister would come to see me", says a woman in the very best of health who has only one way to travel to church and forgets that the minister has one hundred and one ways to travel to reach all his people. I could go on. None of these really answers the question. If only we could get Christian people to realize the meaning of the Lord's Day, how vastly different would be the witness of the Church to the Resurrection of Christ. If you have been guilty of any of these, I plead with you as Christians to look at the Lord's Day and His house in the light of the Resurrection.

You go to church because your Christian life needs Christian strength. If you are to face the trials of tomorrow you must be prepared, by God, for them. You go to church because your Christian soul needs food. "Break thou the bread of life that I might eat and live forever", is the soul's cry to God. We should never depart without being satisfied.

You go to church because your Christian life needs Christian light. How often do the toils and labours of the week blacken your life and drive you to complete despair? How often have you felt like laying down the cause but for the truth that Christ has saved you? You would have given up long ago.

You come to church to have the strength of the spirit imparted and see in the faces of all worshippers the light of Christ.

When that is done we return to the world, new men and women knowing that our way in Christ is the best, and we intend from that witness on the Sabbath, to live on for Him.

BE STRONG IN THE LORD

In the midst of world tension, international mistrust, summit breakdowns and political disorder we are forced to ask ourselves, "Where does the Christian Church stand?" Since we have to live our Christian life in the storm and stress of world crisis and unrest, we do need the certainty of our faith to sustain us and the victory of the Gospel to constantly assure us.

Many of you have been to church this week. You have said your prayers, sung the songs of Zion and listened to helpful and inspiring sermons from your ministers. In a word, you have been well-fed spiritually. The question remains, "What are you going to do with your spiritual abundance?" You are loaded with spiritual ammunition but how are you going to expend it? Not until we stop being targets and become guns — flowing rivers instead of cisterns — are we going to see any change in our world. To be effective we should have something positive to say to the world of men's failures rather than something against their waywardness. As Christians, our calling and responsibility demands that we go into the world of lost men and bring the light of the Gospel to their needs. This, of course, is not easy, for it will leave us soiled and worn, tired and exhausted, discouraged and disappointed. The work of rescue, which has become a lost art, is still the most difficult task that we can set for ourselves.

I believe that we can do much better than we are doing. For most of us, our churches have become monasteries with walls so high, worship so proper, meditation so Godly and instruction so elevated, that in our greed for personal and private devotion, we have absolutely forgotten the needs of those who stand outside perishing for the food we refuse to give and longing for the strength that is ours to instill. If we remove the doers from the Church, those men and women who do all the praying, all the giving, all the teaching, all the work, I do not know what the rest of us would do to retain our religious respectability.

This almost sounds like an undeserved indictment, an unfounded criticism with no basis in fact. Let me ask you, then, as a member of the Christian Church: Who is it that teaches your children in Sunday School? Who is it that leads your young peoples' groups? Who is it that ushers you to your place in the sanctuary? Who is it that gives leadership to the mid-week groups in your church? Who is it that keeps the men and womens' groups going? Who is it that meets regularly the financial obligations of the church? Who is it that organizes your sports programs and picnics? All these things and many others are happening in your church and I leave it to you to be the judge of your Christian stewardship. Are you a weight or a lift? Are you a producer or a parasite? Are you, in the name of Christ, a burning light or just a spasmodic flicker?

Our condition as Christians may be weak but it is not hopeless. It may be ineffective but not dead. "Be strong in the Lord." If we are sick in soul and body, this is the medicine that will surely revive and restore us to our place in Christian service.

To be strong in the Lord, which should be the desire of all Christians, means first of all, the constant exercise of our Christian faculties. Worship is a basic ingredient in our faith. It is those who hunger and thirst after righteousness who will be filled. Many of us are giving too little time, too little care and too little thought to this means of grace. Never forget that we become like the things we worship. If you want to be proficient on the piano, you practice. If you want to become proficient on the football field, you practice. If you want to become proficient on the tennis court, you practice. If you want to become a swimmer, you get into the water. If you want to be a proficient Christian you will have to practice communion with God. Jesus never set forth without seeking heavenly direction. He never experienced an ordeal without waiting patiently before God. His communion was not hurried or impulsive but flowed quietly and daily from a meditative soul. It is in this act of worship, where the soul is tapped in on the resources of God, that we are led toward acceptance, without reservation, our Christian work.

If we have faltered in our labour, you can be sure that our worship has been void of earnestness and continuity. The reason we run dry in our Christian work is simply because we have not taken time in worship to fortify our spirits and the needs of our souls. It is a fact that we need many workers in the Christian field today. We have been spectators far too long. We need to leave the seats of apathy and indifference and become involved as charging participants in the evangelization of our community, our country and the world. There was a time when the Christian turned the world upside down. Today we are leaving the task to the forces of evil. If there was ever a time when the Christian needed to take his coat off and come to grips with eternal realities, it is now. I am sure the incentive is there. All we need is the dedicated willpower. One of the greatest spiritual triumphs that could happen in your parish or congregation is to match your ounce of faith against your ton of doubt. Call upon your minister and ask him for some Christian work to do. While he may be shocked for a moment, he will soon recover and put in your hands the tools necessary to do the job.

In gaining this Christian confidence, you will soon become witnesses for the Kingdom of God. A witness is any man or women, who having seen and found the living Christ, will come in all honesty before the bar of the world and tell what he has seen and found in the living Christ. The best evidence you can muster for such a Christian witness is a dedicated life. Very simply this is what it means to be strong in the Lord.

I cannot conclude without appealing to your Christian heart to be up and doing while it is the day, for the night cometh when no man can work. It is such service that the Lord requires.

THE TOUCH OF FAITH

And a woman came — and touched the border of His garment.
LUKE 8:43, 44

One of the sad tragedies of the age is the decline of faith. Very often the reason given is that it is out of date. It no longer fills the bill. After all, in the material world where change has been so rapid, men find it necessary to adopt newer devices in order to compete with the changing conditions. When we speak of faith we are speaking of something that is never out-of-date, never out-of-harmony with any age and fits into every scheme of life. Faith today finds itself like the inventions of a century ago, out of use, but unlike the inventions of years gone by it still exists for men and women who are willing to live by it and have their lives fashioned after its making.

As we observe the setting of our text and reflect upon those early Christian days, we are immediately struck by the sublime importance that Christ placed upon faith. Here we see a company of men and women following Christ and we cannot help but feel that all were not following Him for the good that He might bestow upon them. Some we would find in that company were following Him out of curiosity. Others were in the march for the loaves and fishes seeking what they could get out of religion without putting anything into it. There was sure to be the Pharisee who sought to question His teaching and call Him to give an account of His authority. There were also the disciples who clung close to hear what He had to say and what new message they could catch from His lips.

In the centre of the throng there was one soul who wanted to look upon Christ, one whose heart was breaking for a glimpse of the Son of Man. One who had a great need that only Christ could meet and satisfy. It is a touching story. I can visualize this poor woman following the multitude for miles trying to break in upon the ranks and being cruelly pushed to one side. Not discouraged she continues to follow in the march. At last, an opening in the ranks, giving her her long awaited chance. Slipping between the crowd that pressed very close to Christ, she put forth her hand and touched the hem of His garment. At that moment the faith became a shining reality. Divinity and humanity had met. The woman became a new person in Christ Jesus. It is important to note that this woman could never have been relieved of her great physical ailment unless she had responded to a faith that drove her to the very presence of Christ.

Many of us today have a kind of faith. Unfortunately, it does not send us all the way. We know that religion is the greatest comfort in all the world but somehow we never think of allowing faith to make it a reality for us. It is very often in the hour of sorrow that some of us learn our first lessons of faith. It is then that we look upon Him who has promised to be our all sufficient hope and to make the greatest darkness turn into light by His holy presence.

No one can really understand what God has for them until they find themselves within the folds of the redeeming Jesus. If we would know the deep secrets of faith we must first come to Jesus and touch Him. By doing that we shall learn what it is to walk by faith alone. It is only in the companionship of the Master that we can ever hope to know what faith has to offer us. It is not enough to know about Christ. It is not enough to pay Him homage in places of worship. It is not enough to be governed by religious precepts. We must get to know Christ personally. We know Him as the personal Saviour of our souls. We must in faith come to Him if we are to have the sins and the great weaknesses of our life met and healed.

This woman had an object for her faith. She wanted to see to Christ that she might touch Him. Seeing Him would not have been enough. She must have that personal contact. This personal faith is always necessary. When we say that we have faith in a person we mean that we know they will never fail us. We can trust them. All men have some kind of a faith. Even in the ancient religions, men and women had faith in certain gods. They believed that they would do things for them but in reality it was necessary for such people to do things for themselves. They had to come with their offerings and lay them at the feet of their gods before they could expect anything in return. This was also true in the case of this woman. She had to play her part and her part was to believe that if she came to Christ He would heal her of her illness. That also must be true of us. We must come to Jesus believing that He will meet us in our great need and by His power remove the guilt of our lives by the touch of His.

Some of us, however, miss the point. We come to Him but in our heart we bring doubt. How can Christ do anything for anyone unless there is first of all in their lives, a belief that He can. We work together in the removing of sin from the core of our being. Like this woman, we must have an object for our faith. Once that has been determined then we must come to the object before it has any value for us. A lighthouse is an object of safety but it is only that to those who come to it and are guided by its rays to places of safety. Christ, then, is the object of our faith. Christ is only of value when men come to Him and have Him touch their lives. To have a living faith in Him is to have a faith in everything that we do and everyone that we know.

Unfortunately, faith is the thing that is missing from our lives today. Somehow we have lost faith in human nature because human nature has lost faith in itself. Our faith has been ruined by many men and women in society today. There are politicians who have told us that they will do much for the betterment of their fellow man when once they have achieved power. Somehow they have not kept the faith. They have lost their nerve and failed to put into action the very thing that good faith sent them to do. Think of the financiers who in faith have taken money away from people and in the midst of the folds of their own selfishness, have sold their faith for a "mess of pottage". Think of the people who have told you that you can have faith in them to help in any enterprise. Somehow that never materializes.

What then is the problem? I believe that it lies not so much in the conditions that surround us, but rather in the careless way we have treated the object of our faith. If we are going to regain faith in mankind and in ourselves we must come and touch the very source of all living faith, Jesus Christ. We have to learn to keep faith with Him before we can ever learn to keep faith with our fellow man. Think on the things that have been accomplished by those who have had faith in God. Behold Abraham, in his old age, going where faith called. By faith, Paul ventured his life to the Gospel, and by faith he was ready to die for it. By faith, our forefathers travelled the unknown seas in search of a new land where they might dwell. By faith, our missionaries have gone to far away fields to give the Gospel to those who know it not.

No one else could understand the meaning of their faith save themselves and the One who had planted it in their hearts. When we come to Christ we do so in faith believing that He can do what no one else can do.

Would that He might touch us, that our faith might bear the marks of real service. That we in this place might have a part in the bringing of the faith of Christ to the lives of others. I want you to know that we must come. No one can provide you with a faith like Christ and His faith will carry you and me into the rich places of His own eternal service.

HE SHALL HAVE DOMINION ALSO
FROM SEA TO SEA

PSALM 72:8

On this Dominion Day it is well for us to pause and recount the blessings that have come to us from the act of Confederation. From small beginnings have come great things until at last we stand out as a nation of distinction. It is important to remember that a nation is made up of people who think and act according to the wisdom that is theirs. Every nation is a product of that action, that ultimately plays a part in deciding a nation's destiny.

Our appeal today is in terms of the relationship of the nation to religion. Our forefathers were very conscious that in order to survive our nation must be built upon a foundation of religion. The democracy that is ours was cradled and reared in religion and without religion, it will come unglued. Our society can only be held together by a common faith in the fundamental nature of man. That is why our nation today must be careful, amidst its material prosperity, not to lose sight of this essential faith. You will observe that the Psalmist was appealing to man's faith in God and to the recognition of that faith as contained in the Word of God. Therefore, what a nation is and what it is likely to become in moral goodness, social advancement and intellectual pursuit will always be contingent upon what is a true essence of its faith.

We must recognize that there have been failures within the framework of our nation and those who have a faith in the Living God must make an attempt to resolve the same. I think it can be said that we claim to be the best salesmen in the world, yet the tragedy is that we have been trying to sell the wrong articles. We have felt strong but we have felt strong for the wrong reasons. We have been telling the outside world about our refrigerators and our production lines but what we should have stressed is the strength that comes from our Christian faith. Objects have not the power to move men's hearts. We need to know that in the long run we cannot be defended by money, or by armies or by technological know-how. Without firm conviction and belief in the Christian way of life verified by experience, we cannot build an enduring nation and defend ourselves against our enemies. The most precious article we have to sell is our faith, yet we have not succeeded simply because we have not believed.

To the Church of Jesus Christ in the nation there is a responsibility that cannot be averted or declined. We need to hear again and again that man cannot live by bread alone and if all that we have is bread to offer, then men and nations will still go hungry. We cannot continue to offer our people "pie in the sky" when all the time what they really need is the God of the Heavens.

We must measure up to our responsibility in terms of our Christian creed. To begin with, the Church must again renew her commitment to Christ and be prepared in the nation to set His standard and His proclamation above ourselves. We must move from the blind alleys along which we have been travelling to the open highways where we sing about the things we believe and where our actions are an endorsement of our faith.

Our responsibility, therefore, in the nation is first of all to give ourselves to the ideals for which Christ died and rose again.

We must be reminded that behind all of this there must be the element of personal and collective sacrifice. The Church cannot survive and do her work with the pittance that her people offer. Without the indulgence of self, nothing can be accomplished.

Then, too, there is the necessity of the missionary enterprise of the Church within the nation, where its task through its people is to call for a faithful trust in God. It is true that this will present hazards and difficulties, but our religion should be something more than "a basket of goodies". Our journey should be measured not by what we take, but what we are prepared to give.

"He shall have dominion also from sea to sea" is the Christian model for this day.

To do our task in the nation it behooves us as individuals to speak in language which modern seekers can understand and to which they may respond. Elton Trueblood puts it this way:

> When we seek to do this, we are engaging in the most practical of human endeavours. There are two practical effects which sound thinking should have. In the first place it should have a direct bearing on the course of events. A people who really understands what they prize, act in ways greatly different from the ways of those who are confused or unconvinced. We must restate the fertile vision in such a way that it may inspire us

to dedication and ultimately to action which alters history. In the second place, such thinking ought to help us to have something on which to fasten in the midst of whatever disasters we, as individuals, may have to endure.

Finally, like the apostle Paul, we must stand fast in the liberty wherewith Christ has made us free. Let us not be entangled with the yoke of our material prosperity at the expense of curtailing our Christian faith.

THE CHURCH'S STAND IN THE MODERN WORLD

We ought to obey God rather than men. ACTS 5:29

The Christian apostle preached these words in one of the first sermons ever delivered in the Church of Christ. It is coloured with a personality that has felt the power of the risen Christ in his life. It reveals the spirit of a man who has lost himself with all his carnal desires in a great adventure of faith. This was no easy task nor was it any wild notion. The very time was against such a conviction. All the religious political forces of the day were directed against such a movement. All planned to kill the movement before it had begun. Since human elements had ceased to exist and human standards had died a natural death, it was an easy thing for the apostle to take his stand even in the face of death. The forces that were against him were secular in their interests and selfish in their motives. They were afraid of losing their own cause. Here we see two forces or powers working against each other: the one Divine the other human.

It mattered not to Peter what men might do to him. They could shut him up in prison, beat him or even take his life. Whatever the cost he was determined to obey God rather than men.

That, my friends, was the spirit of the Early Church. They were not counting the cost so much as they were counting the gain. They stood firm for what they believed and left themselves open to the guiding of the Holy Spirit. Their religion was a living thing. It was something that they were prepared to die for. Nothing human was going to limit its power or narrow its scope. Its message was universal and this gave them length of vision and boundless courage. It was not something that was confined to any one nation. No one could curtail its regenerating force. So the Early Church took their stand for God and contended for the teaching of Christ,

We ought to obey God rather than men.

This calls for the Church to take a very definite stand in the world. From the beginning the Church has shown itself to be a distinct company of people. Right from the start people moved toward the Church. Some out of curiosity; others in the spirit of revolt; still others as searchers of the truth. But whatever the motive was or how indifferent was the approach, the Church broke in upon their souls and molded them into a solemn company.

Is the modern church the centre of similar interests and wonder? Does she manifest the power of the Early Church? Does she show its courage and its spirit of devotion? Does she dare to stand against the indifference of the world, to challenge its sin and bring men under conviction? Does she reveal the same magnetic influence? Are the strains of wonder in her makeup? Do people gather around the altar and cry out from the depths of their souls? In answer to all of these questions, I am afraid we are obliged to confess that the modern church has fallen by the wayside and that multitudes of people remain outside her influence.

Wherein then lies our failure? As I see it we have been placing too much emphasis upon the human worth of the Church and too little upon the Divine. We are constantly asserting what we are going to do and we never make room for what Christ's going to do. The Church has drifted from its lofty spiritual charge and has allowed itself to march in the ranks of the world. It has lost much of its Divine unction simply because it has adopted worldly means to advance its cause. How can the Church ever expect to accomplish its Divine mission and make the House of God sacred, if only on the Sabbath she opens her doors to Christ and during the week opens her doors to the world. It is difficult, at times, to see what the Church is really trying to do. More than once I have felt that she is attempting to make better card players or more accomplished actors out of her membership than she is making saints of the most high God or followers of Jesus.

It is just that very thing that is sapping the heart of the Church and making it a laughing stock in the world. We must break with the world and humanism that has gotten into the Church today. We must obey the voice of God and listen to Him as He calls us on to greater things. The Church's business is the redemption of the world.

Her place is in the world but not of the world. This may not be our conception of the Church and some of you may be offended at the position I have taken, but this is the Christ-like position of the Church and as His disciple and a minister of His Church, I am compelled indeed to see to it that this church is to be kept the sanctuary of God, the House of Prayer and the sinner's refuge. That is to be our stand here and by the Grace of God, it must be maintained.

We ought to obey God rather than men.

This means, again, that the Church must take a definite stand in the affairs of the world. Too long the Church has remained quiet while men and women have been the victims of the worst kind of selfishness. Think if you will of the exploitation that is going on in the industrial world today. Listen, if you will, to the heart sighs that reach us from many homes today because of the lack of work. Behold the youth as they idly wander the streets. How totally indifferent they have become towards religion. Listen to the radical platforms that stand now in our midst contending more for revolution than for peace and order. See how political ideals have been lost in individual selfishness and to what extremes some men will go to obtain the "Almighty Dollar".

Has the Church no part to play in the eradication of these social evils? I tell you, she has, and she must call upon all her powers to see to it that a change is made. If she finds conditions seriously hindering her work; if there are injustices which prevent men and women realizing what they were meant to be; if there are social conditions which make the offer of the Gospel seem a mockery, the Church is bound to do her part with all the great force at her command in the effort to sweep these oppressive conditions out of existence. If the Church finds poor housing and excessive poverty blocking the way of Christ to many in the land, can it be other than her duty to go forward in the strength of Christ and deal with them.

What the Church ought to do, then, in vindicating the teaching of her Master, becomes quite clear. Let her reassert the plain social principles that underline all of the life and teachings of her Lord. Our neighbours are all those who need us and we are to love them as ourselves. The law of the Christian life is the service of the weak and those who cannot help themselves. The poor are the special objects of Christian love. Wealth is a trust and means, not an end. "Whatsoever ye would that men should do to you, do ye even so to them." These are some of the essential ingredients of real Christianity and we need today a new vision of what they mean.

As a Church of the Living Christ, we must expend every effort to put into practice the social ideals of the Master. We must widen His influence and dare to stand for Christ in the social affairs of men. We must obey Him rather than men. If we are ready to do that, our work for the Church here is going to count for something vital.

We ought to obey God rather than men.

There comes to each of us a personal responsibility. It is not enough to know the prevailing conditions of life around us and not see to it that we personally strive to make them better. It is not enough to change the social environment of the man without changing the man himself. It is not working on things and conditions from without that is going to usher in a better and brighter world, but rather it is working from within and setting men's hearts right with God. It is not social reform so much as social regeneration that this world needs, nor is it revolution so much as religious revival that will lead men and women to greater things. We must as members of the Living Church throw all our powers, our talents and our whole being on the side of righteousness. We must stand together for God and proclaim a Gospel that is going to change every facet of human life.

But let me remind you that we can do very little unless our lives testify to the worth of the Gospel. We can never expect to attract men and women to Jesus unless we know Him first as our Redeemer and Lord. We must see that our own lives bear the marks and standards of the spiritual world, before we can have any influence on the material world. We must be able to show Christian kindness to our brothers and sisters in the Lord before we can ever win men and women to the loving kindness of Jesus. There has to be spiritual brotherhood within the Church before there can ever be the brotherhood of man the world over. We must learn personal obedience to Christ before we can ever attempt to call men to personal obedience to the principles of His Gospel. Our own evil and selfish desires must be banished before we would call men to repentance.

Service in an official way or unofficial way in the Church, must be gladly rendered and prayerfully maintained before we can go out into the highways and byways and compel men to join the service of our Lord and King. We must know how to walk the roadway of humility and know how to labour in the front ranks or in the rear, if we would make His Church a place where the feet of the wayward would turn. We must know ourselves right with our fellow men before we can stand right in the presence of God.

All of this is a great challenge to us as it was to the early apostle. It would be impossible if we attempted to work it out for ourselves but ever remember this, "If God be for us, who can be against us." If we are ready to listen to His commands and willing to obey His voice, our tasks will not be so hard or our burdens too heavy to carry. Let us then on the strength of our Lord go forward to make His Church a power for good, not only in this community or in this city, but in the whole land.

That is what Christ would have us do and in Him we have the only remedy for this world of ours. No problem is too hard for Him to solve; no need too great for Him to relieve; no sinner so far from His loving fold but he can win and set him in a high and honourable place among men. If Christ can do all this, and I believe He can, why not let Him lead us in order that the ideals of His Kingdom may be realized in our midst and in the world.

May God give us the courage of our convictions now to surrender our way to Him and our lives to His service.

CHRISTIAN COURAGE

And He said unto them, Why are ye so fearful? how
is it that ye have no faith? MARK 4:40

Everyone admires courage and no one would like to be thought
lacking in it. The Greeks numbered courage among the four
cardinal virtues, yet many people today, if asked to name the
important Christian virtues, would not naturally think to include
"courage" in the list. The very mention of the Christian character
suggests to many minds, only the gentler qualities. The word
"courage" is quite common in the Old Testament simply because
of the prominence of war throughout much of the story. "Be strong
and of good courage, fear not." Courage really comes to the fore
in the books of the New Testament.

To begin with, there was the courage of Jesus Christ Himself.
How is it that so many people have formulated in their minds
such a frail and unheroic picture of Jesus. Perhaps too many of
the hymns they sang at Sunday School gave that impression. It
certainly has no basis in the Gospel story.

What physical courage our Lord had in the face of danger!
When He and His disciples were caught in a storm in a little boat
on the Sea of Galilee, the one person who showed no sign of
panic was Jesus. On another occasion we see Jesus standing up
to a crowd of people in the courts of the Temple and driving
them out because He was indignant at their conduct. Here was
a crowd of people who had religious custom and authority on
their side, being challenged by a stranger amongst them. Jesus took
the law into His own hands and simply drove them out. It was
a most courageous thing to do.

Yet these are insignificant when compared to the moral
courage that He showed throughout His entire life. Taking His own
road; risking everything for the light of truth even in the face of
opposition; not always ready to count on His friends and knowing
that His enemies were always waiting for Him in ambush. He took
the straight road that knew no turns. His friends and His disciples
tried many times to dissuade Him. What He did and what He
said seemed to drive away those whom He was trying to win.
It must have been hard for Him to go along alone against the
world, and let Himself be numbered with the condemned. But

He went on and endured the Cross, despising the shame. Can you think of anyone to compare with Jesus for sheer unflinching courage! He looked neither to the right nor to the left — absolutely undeterred by any wind of popularity as He set His face steadfastly to go to Jerusalem.

It is plain that Jesus' disciples caught something of that spirit of courage from their Master. It did however take time. When they found themselves involved with their Master in public suspicion and legal difficulties, they were inclined to alter their course. When He was arrested, they all slipped away and one of them, Peter, denied any connection with Him. Yet only a few weeks afterwards we find these very disciples, when left to carry on their Master's great enterprise, standing up in the face of all and declaring, "We must obey God rather than men." The authorities were baffled. "When they saw the boldness of Peter and John and perceived that they were unlearned and ignorant men, they marvelled; and they took knowledge of them that they had been with Jesus."

Was there ever a more courageous adventurer than Paul, a man who moved about the world for thirty years without any settled home. Disowned by his people, persecuted almost wherever he went, time and time again being flogged and thrown into prison, and yet going on calmly through it all undaunted, irrepressible, bearing all men's burdens as well as his own.

Whatever other qualities those first Christians may have possessed, there could be no question about their courage. Without courage there could have been no Christianity at all.

The early Christians needed courage but does the Christian life today call for it? Everyone needs courage. At any moment you may find yourself in a situation in which your courage will be tested. Doubtless these situations are more common in some walks of life than others. Our newspapers record daring deeds of courage on a daily basis. But apart from these situations, courage is needed for right and honourable living: the courage of one's convictions; the courage to differ from other people; the courage to take a difficult line; the courage to risk unpopularity; the courage to be alone with truth; the courage to rise after a fall; the courage to let ourselves be guided by neither praise or scorn, pleasure or pain, but by the star of truth. For many of us it is far more difficult to face ridicule and misunderstanding, coldness and criticism, unpopularity and the loss of friendship, than it would be to face physical danger. Yet this most difficult kind of courage is absolutely necessary to go through life nobly and well.

How then are we to question that courage is necessary for the Christian, since the Christian life is the life raised to the highest possible degree? Some people think of it as a "safety first" kind of thing — to be sure of Heaven so to miss Hell — a life lived with the instincts of a flock of sheep in which each one follows the other because all are easily frightened! But is that really the Christian life? Christ calls us to the place of continual danger. Read the Sermon on the Mount and think out its application to the actual world in which we live — about letting your light shine; about being persecuted for righteousness sake; about turning the other cheek; about your attitude to money; about facing life without worry; about seeking and finding. Could you face that unsheltered, uncalculating kind of life?

True courage possesses a moral and spiritual quality. True courage is not the absence of fear but the conquest of fear. This applies even to the courage that remains unflinching in the face of physical danger. It is recorded how General Gordon would stand on the top of the trench with his field glasses to his eyes while shells and bullets were flying around him. His officers begged him to cease such madness and come down at once. There he would stand, as cool as a boy looking for mushrooms, until he had seen what he wanted to see. Did he not know what fear was? Listen to what he said himself, "For my part I am always frightened and very much so." Yet he was an outstandingly brave soldier.

Of course there is such a thing as natural, physical fearlessness. There are people who simply do not fear danger. That is a great blessing. But then, in itself, it is not courage in the true sense. These people may not be very brave in the highest sense of the word. What about one's moral courage, convictions and responsibility? What about the courage that leads one to take a different line from the crowd they happen to be with at the moment? Here we are talking about courage that possesses a moral and spiritual quality to be won in moral and spiritual ways and not by physical endowment. It is not the absence of fear but the conquest of fear. It is not a matter of bodily constitution or of temperament, but of character.

Like other virtues, courage does not come all at once but it grows gradually through faithful practice. It is not by daydreaming about the brave deeds we might do that we shall become brave, but by faithfully overcoming our fears in the little things of daily life.

But how can we do that? What can conquer fear? Ultimately, the one thing that can conquer fear is faith. Faith may exist in many different forms and degrees. There is something of it in any great devotion. It may be devotion to an individual or a cause. Many a timid mother has performed a bold act to save her child. Many a fighter has been made brave by a passionate belief in his native land or in the rightness of the cause which he has espoused. The moral courage that we need every day depends upon our having a genuine faith in righteousness, honesty, purity and truth. In order to have the courage of our convictions we must have deep and strong convictions.

Faith in God is the supreme source of courage. The one thing that can make people brave in all circumstances, lifting them above the fear of danger, suffering and death, above the fear of man, disgrace and isolation is to believe in Christ. Where do you stand in the light of all that has been said? Have you been brave enough, not only to take your stand for Christ but to go beyond that and let Christ have complete control of all your life.

CHRISTIAN HONESTY

It is well to note that three of the Ten Commandments relate to the matter of honesty. It shows us how important honesty is. Although a fundamental virtue, if we follow the spirit of it we are led far beyond the letter of the commandment, to the mind of Christ.

Thou shalt not steal.

Stealing is still common enough, but to most of us it would never enter our minds to become thieves. There are many ways, however, of transgressing this commandment without actually becoming thieves — for example, unfairness, meanness, double-dealing.

Thou shalt not bear false witness against thy neighbour.

This takes us back to a day when it was difficult to get reliable evidence and slander was easy, but we cannot be content with that. The Bible takes a strong stand on things such as gossip in private life and on every kind of partiality and favouritism in public life. The Christian application of the commandment means that we cannot be unjust or uncharitable in our discussions about other people, lest we should play a part in spreading evil about them. There is no sin so deadly as the sin of gossip. When one's character is at stake, remember: Is it true? Is it kind? Is it necessary?

Thou shalt not take the name of the Lord thy God in vain.

This is often taken as a command against irreverence and blasphemy but it is actually a command against perjury. It refers to the custom of giving weight to one's assertions in a court of law by a solemn mention of the Name of God. The giving of false evidence under such an oath is called perjury. It is common for people today who are anxious to apply weight to their assertions, to informally bring in the name of God; for example, "God knows I am speaking the truth", "Heaven is my witness", "As there is a God above", "I swear on a stack of Bibles", etc. Very often it is the people whose word is not particularly trustworthy that are most likely to back their statement by uttering a religious oath. How refreshing it would be if we all had a natural reverence for the truth so that we could be straightforward and expect our "yes" and "no" to be accepted without any tags attached.

To say that we must be truthful seems almost unnecessary among decent people, yet there are many who would not tell an outright lie who, nevertheless, cannot be forthright with their friends and neighbours. What a common thing it is to be a little two-faced in some controversial matter — to avoid disfavour or gain favour with both parties; to change your tune according to the company you keep; to trim your sails according to the wind that is blowing. There are people who will not differ with you in your presence but will differ with you in your absence. It is possible then, to sin against perfect honesty and truthfulness.

One may ask, "Where then are we to draw the line?", since it cannot always be a duty to speak as we think. It is not a matter of drawing the line at all, it is a matter of right spirit and outlook.

In actual practice it is not usually difficult to know what truth demands in our dealings with others. It is useful to ask ourselves: How would I like to be treated? Am I as forthright with other people as I expect them to be with me?

It is not a matter of debating the question, whether it is right in any circumstance to tell a lie. Would it be right, for example, to give direction to a murderer in pursuit of his victim if he asked you which way the man had gone? That may be of interest to the debating society but such exceptional cases do not often arise in daily living. When they do a man usually knows how to deal with them, if he is not thinking of his own convenience but is facing life in a habitual spirit of truth and love.

Many have the idea that we cannot show the same standard of honesty in business as we can among our friends. Necessity, we are told, drives Christian people to practice dishonesty in their business dealings. Curiously enough the old proverb still stands, "Honesty is the best policy". Both of these ideas cannot be true. To a degree, honesty in business does pay, for no man can continue for long in business unless his customers find that his word is as good as his bond. For our discussion, it is not whether honesty is the best policy in a worldly sense. We must be prepared to know that a man may lose heavily through his honesty and we must never doubt that it is worth it, simply because it is not profitable to gain the whole world and lose one's own soul. Jesus calls us to do something better than what we call conventional standards and since it led Him to the Cross need we be surprised that it will involve sacrifice for us.

Christian honesty in business means that we will not only keep agreements but make fair agreements; that we will not turn out shabby work and accept payment for it. If you are a physician it means that you will not give less care to a welfare patient than to a wealthy patient; if you are a salesman, you will not sell anything with the deliberate intention to mislead so that the buyer will discover his mistake when it is too late. Some people will cheat the Income Tax Department though they would never think of cheating an individual or a firm. But Christian honesty cannot allow that distinction.

There are many examples you can draw upon. It is all a question of what we are living for. If we are not living for ourselves but the Kingdom, then we shall do all our work and conduct all our business as servants of Christ, doing the will of God from the heart.

In the final analysis, honesty becomes a very inward matter. "To thine own self be true and it will follow as the night, the day, thou cans't not then be false to any man."

This means that we must have a reverence for truth itself and be honest in all our thinking and believing, even when it is a little uncomfortable. There are times when our accepted beliefs are challenged. Rather than face the issue we close our minds. But we are really backing up when we shut our minds to the things that are challenging, for it is as if we didn't believe in truth. If you believe in truth and reverence it follows that you will be honest with yourself in every matter.

He that doeth the truth cometh to the light.

In the long run the whole matter of honesty, whether in our social relationships, in our industry and commerce or in our thinking, is a matter of being honest with ourselves and with God.

Can we rejoice to know that all things are naked and open unto the eyes of Him with whom we have to do.

CHRISTIAN AMBITION

How often have we heard it said of some youths that they lack ambition? We all have witnessed young people who have moved ahead amid severe handicaps and become successful, while others with excellent opportunities and credentials continue to thrash about in the same old rut. We praise and admire the spirit of ambition. On the other hand, we do not always admire people for being ambitious. We do not like to trust our country's destiny to a statesman who seems to be guided by personal ambition. We do not admire a scholar, writer, social reformer or clergyman whose main motive for action seems to be personal ambition. Anyone to whom ambition is the sole incentive has something rather unsporting about him. The fellow that "keeps the ball to himself" is worth watching.

Ambitions seek various levels. The trouble with many young

people is not that their ambitions are too lofty but that they are not lofty enough. The things they are living for are too base.

Some people are driven by one all powerful ambition in life. Many think to be successful means to grow rich. They assume that the job that enriches a man easily and quickly is the most desirable. Certainly, we must have money if we are to live in this world at all. Once we have obtained our wealth what then do we live for? Christ you will remember, was sorry for the poor but he was sorrier for the rich. It was the people who were caught by the deceitfulness of riches that seemed to Him to be making a very poor go of life. A life that is obsessed with an ambition to be rich, usually becomes narrow, mean, lacking in sensitivity toward humanity, devoid of real happiness, peace and the enjoyment of life. Such a motive is far too demeaning to be the lifestyle of a Christian.

According to our Lord, the only ambition worthy of His followers is the ambition to serve. One day, when His disciples were looking for honour, Jesus told them that to be great in His Kingdom was to be everybody's servant. This means that if we claim to be His, the kind of greatness we shall most desire will not be great wealth, or great power or great honour, but great service — great usefulness in this world of men and women. How does such an approach effect the elements of our lives?

We must come to regard money in a Christian way. Christ saw material wealth as a hindrance to true religion. According to Christ people do not need a great deal of wealth in order to fulfil the true purpose of life. But people do need a certain amount. If we are blessed with much we will regard it as a trust, committed to our care and will use it as an instrument of service. This Christian view of money will affect our giving and make us ask ourselves whether the amount we are giving away to good causes, is in proportion to the amount we are spending on ourselves and on our luxuries.

We shall not regard our work as simply a means of livelihood, an unfortunate necessity, a price to be paid for prosperity. If we have the right spirit we shall look on our work as an opportunity of rendering service to humanity and in that spirit we shall put our best into it. In that generous sense a Christian ought to be eagerly ambitious. It is such ambition that has inspired the best and greatest things that have ever been done.

In many cases, the spirit of service will find its main outlet, not in one's daily routine, but in one's voluntary service rendered in leisure time. Many of the world's good causes depend on such voluntary work. There is plenty of need for the help that young people can give with all the gifts of youth. How many of us volunteer our service to the Church or the community? It makes all the difference whether the work is done in a Christian spirit of service. There is no room for jealousy, petty personal issues and meanness. These elements creep in when people carry on these good works thinking more of their own importance than of the cause they are serving. Christian ambition will teach us something better and would, therefore, achieve far greater things in the service of mankind.

Many may say that this is beyond them. What kind of an ambition then do you want? The ambition that should challenge your life most is the ambition of Christ. The secret of His ambition was found in His obedience to His Father and His personal service to mankind. When we begin to live like Him and for Him, then our lives will never be dull.

CHRISTIAN HUMILITY

Why is it that humility is so unpopular? Why are people so skeptical about this particular quality of the Christian character? Why is it the virtue that everyone praises but few practice or admire? We saw that courage was a quality admired by everyone but not always regarded as having much to do with the Christian life. On the other hand, everyone associates humility with the Christian life, but if the truth were known, few find it attractive. Certainly it is a distinctively Christian virtue. As has often been pointed out, it is in definite contrast with the virtue of "high-mindedness" which was extolled by the moralists of ancient Greece. Among the Greeks, to be humble, was not a virtue. But it is an indispensable virtue in the religion of the Bible, particularly in the New Testament, where it is so closely connected with the teaching and example of Jesus Christ Himself. Yet a great many people pay lip service to this traditional Christian virtue, hesitating to really possess it.

There are a great many people who feel that what we really need in this world is not humility but confidence; not lowliness and poverty of spirit but self-reliance and high-spirited enterprise. "The world will accept you at your own value, therefore, do not think too meanly at yourself. Do not be too humble but go ahead with a good opinion of yourself and plenty of assurance."

This is common advice even among Christians. What then of Christian humility? How can it fit into a portrait of self-confidence and high-spirited youth? Perhaps we have a distorted notion of what Jesus meant by humility.

When Jesus wished to illustrate the spirit of humility He set a little child in the midst. Apparently He saw something in a child which He considered essential to genuine goodness, something which adults seemed to have lost but must repossess if they are to enter the Kingdom of God. Jesus spoke of, "Humbling oneself as a little child". Yet somehow the word "humble" is not one that we would naturally apply to a child. We never dream of praising a child for being humble. What then is the explanation? Perhaps we are misinterpreting what Jesus meant. We commonly think of humility as if it means self-deprecation, low self-esteem, inferiority complex. If that is what is meant by humility, no wonder we do not admire or covet it or associate it with a normal healthy childhood.

An inferiority complex is not an admirable thing. It is a kind of blight from which we should safeguard any child for whom we care. But surely, that was not what our Lord saw in little children. Rather it was that children were simple-hearted and free from self-consciousness — the self-consciousness which sometimes takes the form of morbid self-deprecation, but which may just as easily take the form of self-conceit and pride. There is a passage in the *Idylls of the King* where Percival had failed to find the Holy Grail:

> Oh, son, thou hast not true humility,
> The highest virtue mother of them all -
> But her thou hast not known; for what is this?
> Thou thoughtest of thy prowess and thy sins?
> Thou has not lost thyself to save thyself
> As Galahad.

It seems strange that he should be told that he had thought too much not only of his prowess but of his sins. But we can see that power and sin often go together and that the childlike spirit is different from both. This, I believe, is what Jesus meant. We must be less self-conscious in our goodness. We must learn to think less about ourselves, our own merits or demerits, in our endeavour to live the Christian life. Jesus saw around Him so many earnest people whose eyes were always fixed upon themselves, their own character, their own degree of moral attainment. It is so easy when we are aiming at lofty heights to develop that kind of self-consciousness. Sometimes it takes the form of self-esteem and self-congratulation; sometimes of self-reproach and self-condemnation. There may not be very much difference between the two when it is a matter of being self-centred. Pride may be at the root of both of them. Even the bitterness of self-reproach may be largely the bitterness of fallen pride. There is often a kind of self-worship about it all.

It must have been refreshing for Jesus to turn from that kind of thing to the simplicity and spontaneity of children. Children were so natural. They were not always watching themselves with a self-conscious appreciation. They were so interested in what they were doing that they could forget themselves. They performed kind acts without applauding themselves for it. When they did wrong they did not pretend to be sorry unless they really were and it was not a case of being sorry for themselves. There was neither hypocrisy in it or fallen pride. There was simplicity and freedom from the blight of a proud self-consciousness.

If only adults could be like that. That is what is meant by Christian humility. There is no self-conscious pride connected with it, no false modesty, no self-contempt. The Christian is not lacking in confidence. He does not shut his eyes to his faults and limitations or find it a shattering blow to his pride to face them. He is not afraid to learn new lessons and make new beginnings. Real humility is the very crown of goodness, the grace that makes it universally loved and admired.

Christian humility is based upon the Christian sense of being absolutely dependent on the grace of God. It rests upon the Christian habit of looking away from both our sins and our merits, to Him.

It is important for us to realize that this is at the heart of the matter. While a Christian has to examine himself and repent continually of his sins, it is not genuine Christian repentance unless he looks beyond his sins to God, who is ready to forgive and restore. Sometimes people are too proud to cast themselves on God's mercy and so their very self-accusing has an element of pride in it. They are thinking too much of themselves. Any success that a man achieves in the Christian life is accepted as from God. That is why a good Christian has such a confident spirit combined with the utmost of humility. He aims very high and attempts great things because he is not thinking of himself but of God. He has lost himself to save himself. He is free from all of the self-consciousness which spoils so much goodness because he is so conscious of God.

Pride often involves setting ourselves up because we are not sure of ourselves. This results in our standing so high in our own esteem that we look down in fear of falling. The cure for that is to stand and look up from oneself to God and then fear and pride give way to Christian humility — the heart of a little child.

Even Jesus looked away from Himself to God for His goodness. When an eager soul addressed Him once as "Good Master", He replied, "Why do you call me good? — no one is good except God."

Humility will make us charitable towards other people and that is a vital part of the Christian character. It is easy to be critical, to go about the world dwelling upon other people's faults. It is so easy to withdraw ourselves into our own select circle and talk about others as outsiders, as inferior. All this is terribly un-Christian and it is demonstrating the lack of Christian humility. In our social relationships we often belittle others because we are not very sure of ourselves. We take that route to make ourselves feel important. It gives us a feeling of superiority. It seems to fortify our own virtue. In moral terms, people who are not very sure of themselves develop spiritual pride and the uncharitableness that goes with it.

But all that becomes impossible when we take the Christian attitude of dependence upon God. When we have come to depend upon Him we can no longer be coldly and proudly uncharitable to our fellow man. Then we love because He first loved us. Therefore, when you are tempted to denigrate other people remember what a poor creature you would be if you could not trust in the mercy of God. Then you will be glad to glance away from your faults and the faults of your neighbours' to His great love and to take your place even with the most unworthy at His mercy seat.

> Love the Lord your God with all your heart,
> And ye will love friend and enemy alike.

CHRISTIAN DISCIPLINE

Throughout our study on Christian conduct, we have seen that it is not a matter of merely keeping rules and commandments but having the presence of God in our lives and the spirit of Christ in our hearts. How are we to keep that presence and that spirit day-by-day? The whole story of religion and all the testimonies that come to us from the saints, remind us that it is impossible to live the Christian life without regular Christian discipline of prayer and meditation, fellowship and worship, which keeps the flame of faith burning brightly in our souls.

It is a very old tradition and a very long experience, that tells us that in the interest of religious life, amid the busy activities of the world, it is good for us to keep one day apart from all others. What a sane and healthy custom! It existed in one form among the ancient Hebrews who kept the last day in every week as a day apart and called it the "Sabbath Day". Unfortunately, they came to treat the custom in a far too negative and legalistic way which made it difficult for people to call the Sabbath a delight. Our Lord had to remind them that the Sabbath was made for man and not man for the Sabbath. Later when Christianity began to spread, this custom appeared in a new form. Christians began to keep the first day of the week, not as the Sabbath, but as the Lord's Day, in joyful commemoration of the Resurrection of Christ. They had no difficulty calling it a delight. It was for them the gladdest morning in all the week when they could come together from their daily toil and their pagan surroundings, and worship God in the name of Christ in a warm and joyful fellowship. They could not have carried on without the Lord's Day.

The world has seen many changes since then but in the

twentieth century we still inherit that venerable custom. For us, too, Sunday is a very precious gift and a very special opportunity. Whatever we are going to make of it, it is from the start different from the other days of the week. It is the day on which most do not go to their regular daily work. In that sense it is our own. What use are we going to make of such a precious opportunity?

There is no point trying to answer that question in legalistic terms and declare just what you may do and what you must not do. That is precisely what our Lord disliked so much. In a sense, we have all to answer the question for ourselves. But if we wish to answer it as Christians, there are two things that we must remember.

We must not answer it selfishly as if we had no one to consider but ourselves. Many people feel that the one thing they wish to do on Sunday is to get away from the hustle and bustle of the city and refresh mind and body amid the beauty and clean air of some peaceful countryside. That is a very good thing to do in itself. However, we must make certain that we are not incidently ruining another's Sunday, depriving someone of their Sunday leisure, by spoiling the Sunday peace of some countryside for the people who live there and value it. A Christian must not live for himself alone on Sunday, or weekdays.

We must not forget the health of the soul. If we are looking at things in a Christian way, we know that it is even more important than the health of the body. For the soul's health, Christians have always felt it to be tremendously important that they should, on the Lord's Day give much more time than they can give during the week to think of the things that are unseen and eternal. It is part of the religious discipline by which the Christian life grows and thrives to have this periodic halt in the march of life. This weekly occasion when we can, without haste or distraction, use, in a very special way, the means of grace provided for us by the Christian Gospel and the Christian Church.

Amid the hustle and bustle of our world, it seems far more necessary than ever to preserve that opportunity and to use it well. It is not a matter of keeping an ancient law with a bargaining spirit. It is a matter of asking ourselves as disciples in the school of Christ: What is the very best use that we can make of the one day when the world rests from its labours? It is the first day of the week and it is the Lord's Day on which His people have always remembered with joy, His victory over sin and death. We shall wish to keep it in such a way that we shall be refreshed not only in body but in spirit, prepared to face the week ahead.

A great theologian of our time tells us that the Christian life has, like an eclipse, two focal points: one is the quiet chamber of private prayer; the other is the great fellowship of our Church in prayer.

Religion, is at the same time, the most solitary and the most social thing in human life. When through Christ, it took on more individuality, it did not become less social but rather created the warmest and deepest fellowship the world has ever known. "They continued daily in the temple and breaking bread together — praising God and having favour with all the people."

That is the picture of the early Christian spirit at work. Fellowship and worship working together and from that has come even today the public worship of the Christian Church with its singing, praying, preaching and sacraments.

Do you understand why the Christian life cannot thrive normally without that? Do you see how true it is, that however much we have to stand alone in our religion, we also have to stand together to seek and worship God. No man was ever better at standing alone than Martin Luther. "At home in my house", said Luther, "there is no warmth or vigor in me but in the Church when the multitude is gathered together, a fire is kindled in my heart and it breaks its way through."

Think then of the Church as a great world-wide comradeship of men and women continuing through the ages, from the time of Jesus Christ, bound together by devotion to Him and bearing its corporate witness in every age, as each new generation grows up into its fellowship. When you go to church you go as part of that fellowship, to enter into that heritage and to contribute to it. To share both by giving and by receiving in that religious life of the Church, that river "Whose streams make glad the City of God." How can we create more such fellowship within the Church?

If you try to live the Christian life you will soon discover that it is not enough to worship God publicly with your fellows in the Church on certain days. There must be regular time given to private devotions. Jesus knew how important this was. We see, time after time, Jesus slipping away to be with God alone. He never made a venture without seeking heavenly direction. He never experienced an ordeal without waiting patiently upon God.

Make a quiet time for yourself every day. You may think that you can trust yourself to attend to your devotions without tying yourself to any regular habit. We know that the Christian life can never be reduced to a mere habit and that prayer must not be confined to any mechanical system. It is true that our religion should be hourly and daily if it is true. Yet it is also certain that religion will not be all that to us unless we set aside special times when we can turn our thoughts in a special way to it. Unless we make up our mind to do a thing it is never done.

Set aside a time for your devotions. Make the best use of your quiet time. It is well to have some kind of plan, some kind of definitive direction. A good way to begin is to select some devotional passage from the Bible. This will provide a starting point. Apply what you read to the need in your life and bring all in prayer to God. Think not of yourself in prayer. Remember the needs of others. All this will help you to grow in your religious life.

Be persevering in your quiet time. Nothing is easier than to become discouraged and then one is tempted to become slack. You are almost sure to feel, at times, that it is difficult to pray and perhaps, that it is a useless endeavour. It may be encouraging to know that all Christians and saints have had just that experience; however, those who persisted will tell you that in the end it was all worthwhile. The Lord has said, "Ask and it shall be given you. Seek and you shall find. Knock and it shall be opened unto you." His people have always found that, in the long run, to be more than true.

> Finding, following, keeping, struggling,
> Is He sure to bless?
> Angels, martyrs, saints and prophets,
> Answer "yes".

GOD'S WILL FOR THE CHILD

It is not the will of your Father which is in heaven, that one of these little ones should perish. MATTHEW 18:14

Many years have passed since Christ uttered these blessed words. It would seem that before His time childhood had very little value. His coming to the world gave to the child a new place in society and numbered the little ones as those closest to the Kingdom of the Father.

He had no children of His own but He loved little children. He saw in the child virtues that men and women must possess before they can ever understand the way of God. Jesus goes on to say that unless you become as little children you cannot enter into the Kingdom of Heaven.

In the child, Jesus saw the living model of Christianity. Those virtues of childhood must be ours before we can begin to understand the message and meaning of the Gospel. Their simple faith, their blunt honesty, their noble spirit, their lofty ideas, their imaginative wills, their daydreams and their readiness to mingle with all others irrespective of social standing in this world, are real values in childhood that somehow we have abandoned as we have grown older.

As adults we may disregard the simple traits of childhood. If we read aright the Gospels we are certain to discover that Christ was depicting in the child that which He longed to see in those who had moved into adulthood. It is sad that we have not done a better job of preserving "the child instinct" within us. Of greater concern is the fact that many nations continue to place little value on childhood and the things of children. It is not for us to point fingers and condemn nations for their harsh treatment of children. The fact may be that we have not been diligent enough in sending to them the message of His love. Our own record in Canada is not without blemish. Perhaps one hundred years hence our successors will be ready to criticize us as we are to criticize our predecessors.

In the eighteenth century, nearly seventy-five percent of the children born in England failed to see their fifth birthday. The ideal of Christ was that "Not one should perish". It is our Heavenly Father's will that each one should live.

To bring our text a little closer to ourselves and interpret it spiritually is to call parents to take account of their religious obligations. To present a child to the Lord is indeed a most sacred thing. It must remind parents of a great sacred trust and opportunity that none can afford to miss. It is not enough just to bring your child to the Church and receive its holy benediction, then return home feeling that all is well and your child is spiritually secured.

There are many today who are ever ready to have their children baptized. However, after the rite has been administered they leave and never return to the Church again. There is nothing magical about the act of baptism. As parents we must realize that our responsibility is for the development of the spiritual life of the child. Every opportunity should be taken to advance that spiritual life. It is not enough to pray for your children, you must pray with them. Yours is the task of seeing that children grow up in a religious environment. Your child should see that you love the House of God.

Many are ready to point their finger at the Church and blame her for the lack of religious zeal found among so many young people. Many look at our schools and criticize them for not promoting religious instruction. This is nothing more than an attempt to shift responsibility. It is the home and parents who must accept the responsibility for the apparent religious carelessness that is found among children and young people. Parents are asking the Church and the school to do something that ought to be done in the home. The home is the strongest power in the world for good and it can do more for the Church and the State than any other power that is now in existence.

It is in the home that the child gets his very first impression of religion. It is there the child learns his first impressions of God. For years in the life of a child the parents stand in the place of God. What the child is spiritually, physically and intellectually largely depends upon the influence of the home.

Certainly this is a large task but at the same time it is a great opportunity. If you are faithful to your obligations you will find the Church will meet you and carry forward, to a more glorious completion, that which you have started. However, do not expect the Church to do something in the life of your child that you should do yourself. If you are faithful in your religious duties you will find the Church will not fail you.

As we gather from our text, it is the will of God that every little one should live. We should strive to make that a realization. Fathers and mothers who have little children, who know their love, who see their wonderful affection, who watch as they become a binding force in the home as only little children can do, must be prepared to give them every chance of achieving that for which God ordained.

In the first place, the home should be a religious institution. That is to say parents must be the prime movers in religious education. Father and mother alike must show the same interest in religious undertakings. There must be a common religious understanding between parents before the child can be affected at all. It is a tragedy and one that can only be set right by the love of God, when households are divided on this very question. We cannot expect that the will of God for the child can be achieved under such conditions. Children are quick to notice inconsistencies. When they see mother hurrying them off to church while she remains at home, they soon want to know why. When father spends his Sabbath reading the weekend paper while mother and children are at church, they are quick to ask the reason why. Never on any account ask your child to have pleasure in that which has no pleasure for you. Live with them in the very best atmosphere.

The home must be the teacher of religious truths. I know too well, how difficult it is in this busy world of ours, to practice family worship. I have a feeling that where it is possible it should be observed. When the family is still young and can be brought together easier than when they are grown up, take time to read the Bible together and study its word. This is more easily accomplished when your children are young. In later years, as many of us know, that which we learned about our parents' knees is our sweetest reflection. Every home should see to it that adequate provisions are made for the purpose of religious instruction.

If civilization is to be spared the pain and corruption of paganism, there must be a return to the family altar. Parents, I plead with you now to do your part that the will of God may be realized for your children.

THE REDISCOVERY OF THE CHURCH

Let us work while it is day for the night cometh,
when no man can work. JOHN 9:4

These words of Christ are directed to His followers and to His Church. They could have little meaning in Herod's court or to the worldly crowd on the streets of Galilee. They could have little significance in our materialistic world where men and women are seeking only those things that make them happy for the moment and who have disregarded or discarded many of the finer and better elements in human life.

It is necessary to rediscover the meaning and the purpose of the Church. We are all called afresh to re-examine ourselves in the light of our faith and to see if perchance we too might be numbered among those who may be careless about things that are spiritual.

As Jesus saw it the Church must be a moving stream. It must seek as it moves, to cleanse and purify society and touch the life of man everywhere. The only way that this world can be won for Christ is by every one realizing the importance of their work within the Church and community. As Christians we should be constantly moving forward. We press toward the mark for the prize. We may fall — we may not be able to prevent that — but we ought instantly to regain our feet and to press on with all our moral vigor. Nothing is so dangerous to the Church or to Christian people than to come to a spiritual standstill. A Christian asleep is Satan's greatest triumph!

But our advance must be maintained despite any obstacles that may come before us. You will recall the difficulty that confronted the children of Israel when they were asked to pass through the Red Sea. They were ready to make a retreat but the marching orders of the day were to go forward. The Red Sea became the door for a safe passage toward a glorious Canaan. But I suppose there must be some real conflict, some life and death struggles that we must face. Christianity should not be perceived in terms of taking the easy road ahead. When the call comes we must be ready to fight our way forward. Christ said, "Let us work."

In the first place, the words of Christ awaken us to the urgency of the Christian situation in the world today. Secondly, the words of Christ remind us of the necessity of our personal involvement. Finally, the words of Christ bring to us the light that shines upon the victory that is to be achieved.

What is the urgency of the situation? To begin with, not everyone is Christian. Not everyone is a follower of Christ. Not everyone is a member of the body of Christ. There is a false assumption within the Church today that has greatly retarded our efforts. There are those who feel that the great work of Jesus Christ is nearly done. It is a great pity that such an idea should be held for it is a false conception. It causes us to quiet our conscience and relax our Christian effort. We have been told that not even one-third of the population of the globe are nominal Christians. Less than one-tenth are Reformed or Protestant Christians and out of this small group not much is being realized to advance the cause of Christ. The urgency of the situation today demands that we put ourselves into the mainstream of Christian service where we believe and where we can realize, that our work has relevance in today's world. It must be carried out by those who are God-inspired and Christ-directed.

To do this we must become involved with the needs of our fellow men. We must learn afresh the meaning of love — a love that will project our lives into the lives of others — a love that will redeem us so much that we will not be content until we have laid our hand at least upon one and brought that one into the Kingdom. Jesus, by His coming, identified Himself with a man's need. Can we do less? We must learn to do more.

The formal acts of worship are helpful. They are uplifting. But unless they become as sparks to light the fire in our lives, then little is achieved. We have much work to do and we must share in this work. Involvement, of course, means adaptation — the devising and employment of means needed to accomplish a definite end. One of the most lamentable spectacles of this age is the slipshod manner in which we manage our religious life and display it before the world. It isn't a matter of aiming too low. It isn't that people have no desire for a better life. It is a lack of method and order. A lack of intelligent arrangement.

The world, with its many claims, is too much for them. Even we preachers, whose prime thought and business is religion, have difficulty ordering our lives in such a fashion that our souls can be cultivated for God. Every Christian should bear in mind the words of Paul, "Lest after I have preached to others, I myself might become a castaway."

But to faithful men Christ does finally give the victory, and when this victory comes, thank God we shall see a new ordering of life, where men and nations everywhere, because of our toil and our Christian enthusiasm, will be touched and motivated by the mind and spirit of Christ.

Victories are sweet but one victory leads to another battleground. And so we go on until at last we have reached, in Christ's name, the final victory. As long as we can keep the troops moving forward, there will be victory on our banners. May it be so.

THE CHURCH THAT LABOURS AMONG MEN

Study to show thyself, approved unto God, a workman.
II TIMOTHY 2:15

On this Labour Day Sunday it seems appropriate to take advantage of the occasion to say something that should have a bearing upon our Christian conduct in the everyday world in which we live and make a living.

Quite naturally, there are some divergent views concerning what should be the attitude of the Church in the field of labour and management. There are those who say that the Church should merely preach the Gospel and leave the matter of social questions to the politicians or to the experts in the field of sociology. Others are of the opinion that the Church, as it is presently organized, should be dissolved and that priests, ministers and rabbis should turn their skills to the establishment of a more equitable social order.

I find both of these views very challenging but if we examine them closely we discover that they place upon the sovereignty of God and the Lordship of Jesus, limitations in the creative and saving power of Jesus Christ. We must avoid the extreme of trying to fit Christ into molds of our own making.

I remember coming upon a little shop in Paris where you could purchase almost anything enclosed in a bottle. As my eyes scanned the vast display, I noticed a small bottle that had the figure of Christ encased on the inside. I felt then, as I feel now, that we all have been guilty of shoving Christ into bottles of our own making and putting Him on display in our own little shops and offering Him to the world of men. It is always well to remember that religious and political systems sealed Him into a tomb and went away believing that they had achieved a tremendous victory. Jesus broke that seal and came once more among men to redeem and liberate them from error, superstition and sin.

Let us focus on the work and witness of Christ's Church in the world and review the dangers the Church must face in the world of men. There are attitudes present in the mind of working men and women today that should be of grave concern to the Church. Some feel that the Church has never put a foot forward to assist labour. Others are of the opinion that the Church is constantly in sympathy with management, therefore anti-union. Some view the Church as too neutral — sitting on the fence when grave issues are at stake. Then there are others who are convinced that the Church is more interested in promoting money-making schemes designed to fleece the working public. One man told me that the clergy as a whole lacked courage. They permit themselves to be at the whim of their congregations afraid that if they say or do anything not in keeping with the opinions of their flock, they will soon be looking for another job. One man told me that as far as he was concerned Christianity meant no swearing, no smoking, no drinking, no gambling, avoiding the unsaved and making heaven the only goal.

Certainly these are scattered opinions. However, they give us some idea of the attitudes that may have bearing upon the Church's ability to influence and witness to the working man. Many who labour in our factories, stores, warehouses, shops, mines and in the world of business have rejected any participation in the Church. They believe that Christianity is irrelevant to the life of labour.

The Church must be brave enough to go into this mission field and tell again the story of Christ in language that men understand and through patience and love, seek to capture those who are opposed to Him.

If there is a divorce between labour and Christianity there are things that the Church must do. Each Christian, whether he be a part of management or labour, must rediscover the mind of Christ as set forth in the New Testament.

Even a limited examination of the Gospels will show that Jesus proclaimed a gospel of brotherhood. He gathered His first followers into a social unit with a real communal life. His healing miracles shows His passionate desire to help men physically as well as spiritually. The hardship of the poor was never a matter of indifference to Jesus. Man's material wants were of concern to Jesus. They were written on the heart of God. "Your Heavenly Father knows ye have need of all these things."

The tendency to separate the secular from the sacred was thoroughly alien to Jesus. Christ claimed the whole of life for His province. His Kingdom was to invade every corner of man's experience; every department of public and private life; every nook and cranny of the world. No man was to be able to draw a line to indicate where Christ's authority stopped. We either apply the Spirit of Christ to every human relationship or else drop His religion altogether.

He is Lord of all or He is Lord of nothing. Just as Jesus touched every facet of man's life so should we, as we go to our task, permit His Spirit to have control.

There are some positive signs in our churches that we are gradually coming to grips with men's problems everywhere. In our own denomination, lay people are seeking to discover what relevancy Christ has not only on Sunday but on every other day in the week. In other words, our lay people and ministers must become involved not as professional Christians in the world of work but as co-workers with God among men and women. We may criticize the physical Church but when we come to grips with Christ, Christ grips us.

It should be clear that our involvement carries with it our personal identity with Christ. When the man or woman on the job sees us working, they should also see Jesus.

Perhaps the critics of the Church should be reminded of what the Spirit of Christ has done in the world. The Spirit of Jesus touched the gladiatorial forums and shrivelled that relic of barbarism out of existence. The Spirit of Jesus touched the institution of slavery and laid the ax to the tree that brought it down. The Spirit of Jesus working in Lord Shaftesbury and others, touched the appalling factory conditions of the nineteenth century and put something better in their place. The Spirit of Jesus touched the tragedy of unrelieved pain and distress and everywhere hospitals and homes sprung up.

Always through changed men and women has Jesus challenged the world conditions. We share in this enterprise when into our workplace we bring this spirit. If the socialist cries to the ragged man that his system would put a new suit on his body, Christianity cries out that it will put a new man in the suit.

What are the results to be achieved when Christ is Lord? I challenge any man to point out on the map of the world a place where education, refinement, happiness and purity exists in their highest and best forms without it first being made so by the influence of Christianity. The hands that were nailed to the accursed tree have done more to direct and inspire our civilized world than all other forces combined.

When we know that Christ bends to the lowest and ministers to the vilest and declares that in man, most ignorant and depraved, there is something worth saving, then in His name today and tomorrow, we can go forth and tell men and women that there is no distance between the workbench and the bench of penitence.

Let us match the devotion of this hour with the labour of tomorrow and we will get results. The test of our religion is what we are at home, at school, at play and at work.

Go labour on, spend and be spent.

BE YE DOERS

Church work, like any other, requires time and patience. The old proverb still brings with it a great deal of truth. "You get out of anything what you put into it."

Go back to the Scriptures, always a safe guide, and reflect on the text. James had good reason to use these words. He was writing to people who were obsessed with the then prevalent idea of the coming of Christ. As a result they pulled in their Christian oars. Why push on? Why head out upon unknown waters if the end is so near? Why not just sit down and wait? Why bother about the world? Better for us to meditate upon the good things. Feed our souls at the fountain of easy access. Self-satisfaction brings deterioration. Man is either moving onward to his possessions or he is moving backwards to his ruin. We cannot go in two directions at the same time.

One would imagine that time would teach better behaviour to the Christian Church and that the eyes of our hearts would be opened so that we would never walk or act in the ways of our fathers. The fact remains that we are still troubled by the failures of the past. True advance can be seen in the fields of scientific endeavour but morally and spiritually, advancement has been retarded by the weight of sin which more often than not, wears the garments of self-satisfaction.

The urgency, as one sees it, calls for an awakened faith. A faith that will enable us to cast off the rags of moral respectability and accept without flinching the standards of our own Christian faith. This rightly begins in the sanctuary of our own hearts. "Let a man examine himself", is the first step to an awakened faith. Possibly our greatest weakness in the Church today, certainly the most obvious one, is that we have too many spectators and not enough players. Too many who are content to listen and too few with an active faith.

It is heartening to know that such a condition need not prevail. We can still thank God to change our failure into vital success. The Kingdom of God with its challenge and with all its blessings can be inherited by us all.

I humbly suggest the way to a victorious Christian faith is found simply in our willingness to work with God. Many are the testimonies that tell of the victory achieved by men and women in all walks of life who have committed ownership of their lives, their talents and their time to the work of God.

Here is the challenge to us. As a Christian am I doing anything worthwhile for the Kingdom? Am I giving any of my time to the promotion of the truth? Are my talents on the altar of God or is the world, the flesh and the Devil stealing that which rightly belongs to God? These are some of the things as Christians we are called to confront. Our answer to them will provide much food for thought and will no doubt furnish us with the perfect measure of what we sometimes call our Christian faith.

I ask you to think through these thoughts as a member of the Church. How would you answer God? What kind of a member of the Church are you? I fear the question most when one day I may be asked, What kind of a Christian minister have you been? Somehow this should drive us to the place of prayer and spiritual enquiry.

It should make us more loyal and devoted to our place of worship. Apply all this to the whole work of our church and I think, if we are sincere, there can be but one outcome — a revival within our midst. I pray God that as we go into our fall work that we shall go at it together. Workers, together with God, will make us a strong spiritual people; a people, a church, that will have something to give to those who stand in the need of Christ.

THE CHRISTIAN CONSCIENCE

Pray for us: for we trust we have a good conscience, in all things willing to live honestly. HEBREWS 13:18

Sometimes we forget the part that conscience plays in Christian living. It is one of the strongest powers in human life, whose function and ministry must not be neglected. It presents itself always in terms of Christian conduct. How shall I act? How shall I decide between several courses of conduct? How can I choose between right and wrong? These are the questions that sometimes perplex the mind. Nevertheless they stimulate the conscience.

If we had nothing more to do than to look after our own private life, we could manage quite well. However, the moment we step out into the world we become involved in a public life of battling contradictions. We may know how to act in our own home, or within the confines of a church of like-minded people. The important question is: How shall I act? What shall be my standard of behaviour in the world? What will be the standards of ethics and morality that motivate my Christian living? What support do

I find for these things in a world so full of complex situations where I am not always my own master? How can I carry my ideals into a world that has no ideals?

The writer of the Book of Hebrews points out that a good conscience must be part of our Christian baggage. To keep one on the track and to develop one's character depends on the kind of treatment one gives the conscience. A good conscience is much like a good clock, if you treat it right you can pretty well count on it. If you tamper with it — take it apart and put it together again and perhaps lose some of its parts — you will never be able to depend upon it. Let us, therefore, look at some of the things we must do if we are to fulfil the message of our text.

To begin with I would suggest that we keep the conscience alert. A man numbed by liquor or narcotics is in no condition to co-ordinate mind and body and therefore drive a car safely on the highway. If a serious accident does not occur when the road is clear, he is almost certain to injure himself and others when the traffic becomes congested. So, too, conscience can become sluggish or dull through the intrusion of other things.

Many of us can look back today and see where we got off the track and how we have forever lost the harvest of our hopes, because of our stupidity or because we could not come to a decision. Our conscience faintly whispered the right way but too many other things interfered. It may have been indifference, apathy or carelessness. Unless the conscience is kept alert, it is difficult to measure the harm to oneself or to others. This is why it is necessary to bring our conscience under the influence of Jesus. The moment we seriously turn our thoughts to the life and words of Christ, our ideals of duty become clearer and sharper. We discover a right and a wrong in areas that previously did not concern us. As one begins to understand what is meant by honest dealing with oneself, one can understand how necessary it is to keep the conscience alert.

I believe the conscience must be kept true. When Admiral Perry returned from the North Pole he picked up a peculiar kind of rock and put it aboard ship. As the ship moved out to sea it was discovered that the needle of the compass was being deflected and the ship was moving away from her course. Casting about for the reason, Perry discovered that the rock possessed some magnetic quality which was affecting the compass. It was thrown overboard and immediately the ship found her true bearing.

While conscience is a moral compass for the voyage of life, it likewise may be deflected and warped. Many launch forward on the great world's ocean like a fine vessel, fully equipped for a sure way through the winds and the waves. The conscience is alert to a favourable degree but at one port or another, they have taken onboard something that contains in it an element of risk. Perhaps it is an eager passion for praise. Some people do not seem to get on well without praise. Perhaps it is a desire for some high position. Maybe the climb up the social ladder has consumed their time and attention. Maybe it is the secret craving for some form of self-indulgent pleasure. There is not a person who, if you should sit down and analyze the reason why he has lost the edge of his conscience, could not find something which he has taken unto himself which ought not to be there.

We can only be kept on a true course when we take our bearings from Jesus. To keep the conscience true we can exercise a few minutes each day of self-examination. Very often this can be done by recalling a great hymn. It can be done by bathing oneself in a majestic passage of literature. It can be done by observing the lives of great personalities or by noticing the true course in life which your nextdoor neighbour is pursuing.

Yes, to have a good conscience void of offense one must keep it true. Having an alert and true conscience leads us finally to know that we must have a conscience that can be trusted. But that does not mean that we will not make mistakes. However, when we do, we will have conscience enough to reprove us, to make us back-up to take another start. That is what we mean when we talk about being led by the Spirit of God. The only way that we have of knowing that the soul is in good condition is not by some external sign, but by some inner conviction. I think James had it in his mind, the true meaning of a trusted conscience, when he wrote: "If any of you lack wisdom let him ask of God that giveth to all men liberally, but let him ask in faith, nothing wavering, for he that wavereth is like a wave of the sea driven with the wind and tossed. For let not that man think that he shall receive anything of the Lord. A double-minded man is unstable in all his ways."

The conscience, to be trusted, must depend entirely upon the guidance and promptings of the Holy Spirit. It needs to be said firmly to every Christian within the Church today that we must have these qualities of conscience if we are to make any impression upon the world of indifferent men and women. If the sinner is to see anything of the Christ-like qualities in our lives, it can only happen when we practice the art of developing a good conscience.

If any contribution to the Christian faith and Christian Church is to be achieved we must possess a good conscience. I often wonder how we feel in our conscience when we know that Christian duty is a common enterprise, yet we stand idly by and let others in the Church share the load. How does our conscience act when we know that we are not giving of our time, our talents and substance like others to the cause of the Kingdom of God? What kind of a reaction do we get from our conscience when we have to decide whether to go to church or to stay at home on Sundays? When matters of right and wrong come up within our family circle or workplace, in what direction does our conscience guide us? Do we stand for that which is right or do we compromise? Do we unflinchingly show by our attitude that we are a Christian or by our total indifference permit wrong to be practiced? Do people detect that we have a conscience and because of that we stand for that which is right and honourable and true, or do we take no stand and allow matters to take their own course?

Ultimately all of us must answer to God for our actions. The Christian needs a good conscience, the Church needs a good conscience, the state needs a good conscience. There is an agony in the heart of Christ that can only be removed when we have a good conscience in all things, willing to live honestly.

GETTING A GOOD START

They brought young children to Him, that He should touch them.

MARK 10:13

This was surely an imposing sight. I only wish it could be re-enacted before our eyes, that we might learn well its lessons. There is a common aversion today, much stronger and more obstinate than that which was exhibited by the disciples, to the bringing of children to Jesus. For all such stupidity there comes that strong rebuking word of the Master, "Let the little children come unto me and forbid them not, for of such is the Kingdom of Heaven." Children have many royal claims that no one has any right to deny.

The first thing that I would like you to notice is that these mothers brought young children to Jesus. The Greek term has a wide range of application. It may mean either children of tender years or boys and girls of elementary school age. But in any case, the truth remains that these sons and daughters of Salem were brought to the Saviour early in life. It is the height of folly for any father or mother to allow their children to drift with the world for twelve or fifteen years and afterwards seek to make of them religious prodigies. It simply cannot be done unless the Grace of God has somehow mysteriously intervened. If goodness is sought at all for children, it is absolutely imperative that they should get a good start. The best possible start we can give our offspring is to bring them to the hallowed presence of Jesus. One of our foremost educators has declared that, "This is a generation in which parents are permitting their children to grow up as moral and religious weaklings."

Many people believe that we should let children wait until they are grown and then choose their own religion. If we parents have any desire to keep the weeds out of the hearts of our children's lives we must lead them in their early years to Jesus and let them learn to do His will. In later years it will not be so easy and the souls we love may be lost. We are told that, "they brought their children to Jesus." They did not send them or entrust them to the company of a friend. These mothers themselves brought their little ones to the Lord. They wanted their children to be influenced by Christ. Many mothers today feel the same way and follow the same example. However, there are others who compel their children to go to church and Sunday School, yet stay away themselves. They encourage their children to pray and read their Bibles and practice distinctive Christian virtues, yet these things have no place in their own lives.

This attitude carries with it short-comings and rarely is the objective attained. We have no prescriptive right to ask others to go to a place where we will not accompany them, or to expect them to seek the light that has no pleasure for us. No one will tumble to that quicker than our own children.

If we want them to come and abide under His holy influence then the only safe course for us is to bring them to Jesus ourselves. This has meaning deeper than words. It means that we must ever be careful how we live. Little children are quick to notice inconsistencies and they will be certain to make comparisons of the life we laud and the life we lead. Ungodly parents very seldom have Godly families. If we actually crave our children to be Christian, it is the wise thing to do to set a good example.

Such an example carries with it certain implications. It implies that we must be cautious not only in what we do but in what we say. I do not know of anything that has such a profound influence in turning young people against the Church than the manner in which we speak of religion. Everytime we talk lightly of the Church; everytime we resort to hostile criticism of the Gospel, sermons and music; everytime we mimic and ridicule believers within earshot of our household, we are making it more difficult for our boys and girls to turn towards Jesus. All things pertaining to the Kingdom of God should be esteemed as sacred. If we find something we cannot praise we should at least hold our peace. It is better to err on the side of tolerance than to breathe a single thought that will prevent a soul from looking to its Saviour. After all the centre of our religion is Christ and no one can find fault with Him.

"They brought young children to Jesus that he should touch them." Not that they should touch Him but that He should touch them, and touching here is the matter for a personal and redeeming influence. The highest development always come to us through contact with something loftier and nobler than ourselves. A child's best chance of growth lies in associating with people already grown. If you want him to be a poet, do not point him to the model of the village prankster. If you would make her a topflight physician, do not shut her up in some isolated community where she has no competition. Point children to the greatest and let them mingle with the best. Those things inferior will not do. Those things of equal proportion will not do. Those things a little more advanced will not do. If we want children to make any progress we must point them to the model at the top of the tree. Let them climb for the highest apples even though they may fall in the process. The highest has more in common with the lowest and exercises the greatest power to uplift and to bless.

These mothers of the Gospel story knew that and hence they brought their children to Jesus that He should touch them. They somehow felt that under the influence of the Lord all the loveliness and charm of childhood would be preserved and carried over, with an added glory into the realm of manhood and womanhood. There is the story of the mother who prayed beside the cradle of her sleeping babe, and while she prayed she dreamed and saw messengers drawing nearer to offer strange gifts. One said, "I am Health and whom I touch shall never know pain or sickness." Another said, "I am Wealth and whom I touch shall never know poverty or want." Another said, "I am Fame and at my touch the child shall rise to a place beside the immortals." And still another, "I am Love and at my touch at the darkest hour a friendly hand shall be outstretched." And last of all came one with furrowed face and hollow cheeks and burning eyes, who offered not health nor wealth nor fame nor love but only this, that he could cause the child to love his ideals and never lose them. "This is my gift", said he, "his ideals shall be real to him." And then the mother kneeling down grasped the meaning of that message and cried out, "Touch, O touch, my child."

This must be the plea to the Christ of all parents who seek for their children the eternal fragrance of the flower of character that fades not away. Parents today, parents of this hour, parents of this generation, I beseech you to bring your children to Jesus. I speak not in the name of churches. I speak not in the name of creeds. I speak not in praise of religious revivals. I speak in the interest of the school teacher, in the interest of education, in the interest of social development, in your own interest and for the welfare of your family. The mothers of Jerusalem made a shrewd choice for their model. They came not with their children to Peter or James or John. They sought not to be inspired through Andrew and Philip. They went to the highest, they went to Jesus. Mothers of Canada, parents of Canada, be not less shrewd than they. Would you kindle the inspiration of your children? Beware then of the torch that you bring them. Do not say that here are very small lives and therefore very little will do it. Do not leave them to a match, a taper or a candle. Small lives need the greatest heat to fan them into flames. Seek for them nothing less than the sun. Bring them into the presence of Jesus. They will learn all things from Him — the beauties of the field, the pity of the heart, the fervour of the mind and the charm of the soul. No one else but Jesus is confident to lift them to the very highest and make their characters firm and steadfast.

Let us make this a day when all families together come to Jesus that we might be touched by Him and in this touch find new life, new hope and new strength. Let us in all Godliness go forth permitting Christ to be our power. By our daily conduct let us emulate His Spirit so that all will be well. It is not just character that God has given us to develop but also the soul. God give us strength, courage and patience to carry forth this task today.

ARE WE SURE OF GOD

God, who at sundry times and in divers manners spake. HEBREWS 1:1

Our greatest need today is the sureness of God. Great doubts have been cast across the heart of civilization in this past century. Wars have brought men into the worst kind of conflict. I am not thinking of the bloody assault that shot and shell wrought upon human lives but rather the tremendous doubt that is left upon the minds and hearts of men as to the existence of God. The disillusionment that arose from the battlefield is something that we will always have to contend with. In addition, there is the unparalleled advance in the knowledge of nature with its many scientific discoveries. This idea of progress has tended to create doubt, making religion and God unnecessary factors in human life. Modern religion tends to bring people to a place where they do not care whether they believe in God or not. It puts itself behind closed doors and invites people to feed upon its formula. All it seems to seek is its own selfish security. It is not challenging the heart of man and so sin goes unarrested.

There are many who want to be sure of God. Sure of His fatherly interest in them. Sure that He does care for their eternal welfare. There are those who need to be reminded that there is a God. He does not hurl Himself at men and push them into the Kingdom. Nevertheless He speaks and when He does man must always take account. How does God speak?

First of all God speaks through nature. There are few of us on warm days who have not had our brows cooled with a refreshing breeze. Others of us, who have been confined to the city, are able to get away to some northern lake where refreshing waters give us a new lease on life. There are men and women who have not known what it is to have a single day's fret and toil smoothed away by the peace of the sunset. God speaks through nature but ofttimes the most effective spiritual voices of nature are the whispers of the Lord. An eclipse of the moon reminds me of how God does things. There is no storm, no crashing of clouds, no gales — there is a calm stillness — and in the quiet of it all as one gazes up into the heavens to behold the wonders of nature one can hear the gentle voice of God.

One night Robert Bruce, discouraged and disheartened by repeated defeats, reached a solitary hut under whose thatched roof he tried to find rest until morning. Throwing himself upon a heap of straw, he lay upon his back with his hands placed under his head. As the morning dawned, he gazed at the rafters of the hut disfigured with cobwebs. Forgetting for a time the apparent hopelessness of the enterprise in which he was engaged and the misfortunes that he had encountered, he watched one of nature's smallest insects, a spider, trying to swing itself by a thread from one rafter to another. It failed repeatedly. Twelve times did he notice its unsuccessful attempt. Not disheartened by its failure it made the attempt once more and lo the rafter was gained. "The thirteenth time", said Bruce springing to his feet. Nature spoke to him and the voice he heard was the voice of God, so he ventured oncemore into the struggle for the independence of his country. Success crowned his efforts and it is said that he never once more met great defeat.

Outside my window is a tree. A few months ago it was bare and dead looking. It seldom got my attention, but now it is alive with foliage and is a shelter for singing birds. Nature has transformed it into a picture of life and it speaks to me of the wonders of God.

Last spring as I stood looking up at one of the largest

mountains in British Columbia, I could see nothing but snow-capped peaks. Everything seemed bare against the golden sunlight. Later on in the summer, I stood in the same place. This time my eyes fell upon the same mountain but it had been transformed. In the place of bareness there was life in abundance. Green trees were swaying in the noonday breeze. God had touched that mountain and made it live.

If only we but stop and listen we shall behold God — in the majesty of the stars, in the wonder of the woods, in the warbling of the birds. Listen then, for the voice of God as He speaks through nature. From it we shall learn to believe in a God who lives and works for the glory of this world.

God speaks through history. When God intervened in human history in the person of His Son, the first utterance of His voice was that small cry of a tiny babe barely audible beyond the doors of a rude manger in which He lay. When God, through His Son, intervened in the history of sin the last cry uttered by the Crucified Redeemer barely reached the walls of Jerusalem. Yet the whisper of God betokened a redeemed world.

When Stephen lay dying his shining face sent the whisper of God into the heart of Paul and sowed the seed of conviction in his soul — a soul that burst forth to honour Christ among the Gentiles. When God intervened in the history of the Early Church and spoke through His servant Peter at Pentecost, men became sure of Him and many souls were added to the Church. When God intervened in the history of the Reformation, the dark ages became bright because truth was revealed and the liberty that it bestowed upon men and women made them sure of Him.

When the Forth Bridge was being erected to make a passage way for the railway from Edinburgh northwards, it is said that through some slight miscalculation the last girders would not quite meet. The bridge was left while men went and thought the problem out. One quiet Sabbath day, when the sun was blazing down upon the bridge, a watchman going up and down the newly finished structure found that the sun had expanded the girders and that the rivet holes and bolt holes were, for the moment, in line. Without wasting time, he got the heavy rivets and heavy bolts and knocked in as many as he could. Over the calm river on that sunny Sabbath morning might have been heard the faint hammering that put the finishing touch to a great bridge.

On the hill of Calvary there was heard the faint clang of a hammer upon nails. A hammering that finished the Bridge across which the world is moving out of sin unto God. When God intervened in the history of death and brought to the world a message of Everlasting Life, the first indication of the Resurrection that came from the lips of the Son of God was a whispered word to a woman. "Mary, Mary." He did not shout aloud His triumph nor was His voice heard in the streets.

When God intervenes in human history He does so with the still small voice. God speaks in the hush and quietness of human life, but what I want you to know is that He does speak. His voice, however, can only be heard by those of us who wait on Him. This is the only way that we can make ourselves sure of God.

Finally, I would say that God speaks through the human soul. This is where God becomes our greatest reality. It is in personal contact with God that man learns his first lesson of the sureness of God. Think of Augustine before he became a saint. A voice spoke to him one day as he was sitting in his sin reading the Scriptures, "Let us walk honestly as in the day not in chambering and in wantoness." As he read it seemed that the shackles had fallen from his life. He was made free by harkening to the voice of God in his soul.

One day many years ago I was very discouraged in my work. I was doing a lot of preaching. I was telling people that if only they would come to Christ He would change the sin in their lives no matter how black it was and convert it into purity and goodness. But somehow I was seeing no fruits for my labour. One day in my discouragement, I took a walk along one of Ontario's northern lakes. Sitting down on the bank, feeling depressed in spirit, I happened to look up. My eyes fell upon a lovely lily growing by the side of the bank. I was struck by the beauty of the flower. As my eyes left the flower and wandered down the stem, I noticed that it was growing out of a dark muddy substance. It suddenly dawned on me that if God could take of that mud and make this perfect lily, could He not do more for the sin of man?

I left that quiet lake a changed man, believing more firmly in the power of Christ to change lives. God had spoken through the human soul and I was made more sure of Him.

God has something to say to each of us. His every word is life to those who are willing to listen to His message. There is but one way that we can be sure of God and that is to listen to His voice as He pleads with us to turn from our sin and live unto righteousness. May He give us the attentive ear that we may hear and as we hear may we, with open hearts, receive His only begotten Son as our personal Saviour.

> God calling yet shall I not hear?
> Earth's pleasures shall I still hold dear?
> Shall life's sweet passing years all fly,
> And still my soul in slumber lie?

> God calling yet I cannot stay;
> My heart I yield without delay:
> Vain world, farewell, from thee I part;
> The voice of God hath reached my heart.

OUR SONG OF THANKFULNESS

Be ye thankful. COLOSSIANS 3:15

I am sure that none of us would like to think that Thanksgiving is something that should occur only once in the year in the life of a nation or its people. Since we are daily robed in the beneficent goodness of God, surely thankfulness should be the constant anthem of our soul. The apostle here is exhorting us to remember the place of thanksgiving in our lives. Because we live in the constant danger of forgetting from whence cometh all good things, there are times when we are not as grateful as we should be.

First of all to be thankful is an imperative duty. Every true virtue must be cultivated from within in order for it to be rightly ours. It is to be the product of the will; the result of our self-conscious intentional life. Thankfulness puts us into a right attitude with God. Every true man contributes something of goodness to the collective life of humanity. Every day we are receivers of channels of goodness. Hands are stretched out towards us everywhere, bringing gifts.

To be thankful should be the permanent attitude of our souls to a common condition. The man who offers us some new thought or creates some new object of beauty, or sings for us some new note of melody, or penetrates with deeper skill the depths of nature, or finds some untrodden path in the world around us, that man should win our gratitude and love. Man must have a deity and if he fails to find it in the beneficent Creator, he will put himself forward and pay homage to his own egotism. Many people have difficulty saying 'thank you' to God. God save us from such a spirit! The worship of self is the lowest form of expression to which the human soul can fall. Let us offer praise to God and bless His holy name.

Thankfulness enlarges the blessing received. Gratitude is microscopic and magnifies the insignificant. It broadens one's very countenance to say 'thank you' and mean it. The stars have a deeper shining to the souls who look with appreciation upon their glowing orbs, and to such a mind, stars speak as well as shine. Thankfulness becomes sympathy in the presence of need. Grateful people are usually the most generous. The spirit modifies the evils of life and magnifies its good. It finds the sunny side of the street and from the fragments of passing joys makes a continual feast. How much good we all might find if we only seek it with open, sympathetic hearts.

Then, too, thankfulness prepares larger gifts. It expands not only the gift but the receiver. The appreciative spirit is always helpful to a larger fellowship and a fuller life. Many times you have heard people say, "I love to do something for those people. They are always so grateful." The good in life cannot be enjoyed by the unthankful. Ingratitude chills your sympathy into ice. These unthankful people carry with them the air of the polar sea. They see the somber side of sunlight. The decayed petal is more prominent to their vision than the beauty or perfume of the rose. The golden means of life brings us to the sweet appreciation and contentment of existing things. To be thankful for what we possess is to heighten the meaning of life in suggestiveness and value. Even narrow surroundings intensify the blessings that are possessed if the spirit be praiseful. We have found people whose restricted areas of usefulness and power did not for a moment hide from them the joy that lay within their reach.

Another thought is this. Thankfulness enables us to see in every condition, some element of permanent good. We have sorrow in the world and days of sadness when the sun refuses to shine and the clouds hang low. We must learn to be thankful for winter's chilling breath as well as for summer sun. We can only appreciate the one as we experience the other. Life is full and strong only as it alternates. The picture is beautiful only when the lights and shades balance each other. To fall is the only way to walk. To know the depth we must measure the height. To be patient under life's afflictions is the only way to appreciate health. The losses of life lead to its greatest gains. Let us be thankful that God has granted so much of good.

I think again that thankfulness best shows itself by sharing the good we receive. In the Jewish Feast of the Tabernacles, the rejoicing people were to carry provisions to those who had nothing. Thanksgiving was to interpret itself by beneficence. Grateful gladness was to remember the needs of the unfortunate. To share our good is the first impulse of the thankful heart. No true life can enjoy its good alone. The blessings of God are not to be hoarded but to be distributed. Thanksgiving to God means generosity to men. Many men have confessed that they never knew the good of their riches until they began to give them away. We are to be fertile streams not stagnant cisterns.

To awaken thanksgiving in others is as much a duty as to be thankful ourselves. This can be best illustrated by the story of an old woman living in a small room in the city. A caller said to her, "You never see the sunshine in this north room do you?" The woman replied, "The sun never shines in here but I can see it shining on my neighbour's windows." I am afraid too many of us are like the man who was an incurable grumbler. He grumbled at everything and everyone but at last the minister thought he had found something about which he could make no complaint — the old man's crop of potatoes was certainly the finest for miles around. "Ah, for once you must be well pleased", said the minister with a beaming smile as he met him in the village street. "Everyone's saying how splendid your potatoes are this year." The old man frowned at him as he answered, "They're not so poor, but where's the bad ones for the pigs." Too good to be satisfactory.

This is an hour when we should pause for a few moments to reflect on whether all that God has given us has been wisely received, wisely used and wisely distributed. We are at all times His stewards and as such we must see to it that we make a proper return of His gifts to advance His cause in His Kingdom. Stewardship is part of thanksgiving and if you have found yourself the recipient of all the goods of God and have kept them to yourself, then you are not a good steward. You are like the man who kept his talent buried when he should have invested it.

Thanksgiving is such that it challenges us all to invest what we have for God. The great things in life cannot live except they are sustained by the gifts of God's children. The social agencies need our help. The Church cannot do its work when only twenty percent of its people are good stewards. What then should be our attitude today? Are we thankful as Paul would have us be. As the Psalmist said, "O, that men would praise the Lord for His goodness and for His wonderful works to the children."

This, I believe, must be the measure of our thankfulness. I would ask you, "Have you thanked God for all that He has done for you?" Let us think about our homes, the welfare of our children, the fellowship of our friends, the power and influence of the Christian Church. Then above everything else, what about answered prayer? Surely we must thank God that He has heard our prayers and has brought us safely through some of the sad vicissitudes of life. May God in Christ make us thankful this day.

Hear our prayer of Thanksgiving
O God, for all thy goodness
And loving kindness shown towards us
Since last we assembled ourselves to worship thee.

We are grateful for all the things
Which made our lives comfortable and happy.
We thank thee for the many
Who served us during the week.

Those who provided our tables with food
And those who made the things we wear and use.
Those who have written out their thoughts
For our inspiration.

Those who have entertained us with their songs.
In being debtors, we feel that we must

Render more than pay, if we would
Express our thanks to thee.

Accept our thanks for all the relationships of life,
The passing contacts with people
Which make life interesting and varied,
The friendships which enrich.

The kinships which satisfy our hearts with love.
Bless the strangers who have sought
This house this day.
All we ask is in the name of our Lord and Saviour.

THE GOD WE TRUST

Some people have as much trouble with their religion as they have with their ulcerated stomachs and for the same reason — they just won't follow their doctor's orders. They refuse to diet.

Everytime you come to a service of worship, in theological terms, you are really attending a diet of worship where the Great Physician of life orders the sustenance required by your soul and body. God knows the hunger of your heart, the disabilities of your life and the desires of your mind. What we need to do is trust in God. To get anything out of your faith and to get anything helpful out of a service of worship, there must be on your part and mine, that simple belief that God is the rewarder of them that diligently seek Him.

Did it ever occur to you that many come to worship to find fault with God? To blame God for the poor week they have had. To scold Him for the things He has permitted to happen to them or to members of their family. Each of us arrive here with our burden and doubt but before we are prepared to listen to God we want God to listen to us. We want Him to pay strict attention to our needs. In other words, we haven't come to give. We have come to get. We come like a rebel instead of a recruit. We want to know why a God of love should so mercilessly destroy the plans we so meticulously made for our lives, our homes and our businesses.

It reminds me of the young soldier who found himself caught up in heavy fighting where objectives to be taken remained unreached, casualties were mounting and the hope that had sent him into battle was beginning to fade. In his frustration, he turned to his comrade and said, "Whoever planned this show didn't know what he was doing." There are many people who go around blaming God for mismanagement of things and people, while refusing to accept responsibility themselves. Many a good Christian venture has been scuttled by good people who thought they knew more about running God's Church than He did. The progress of the Kingdom is not retarded by sinful men, so much as by seemingly goodly people, who keep God confined to human rules and regulations. They bottle Him up in theological jargon. Their trust in God is measured only by their own standards. If God gets at their plans and wants to change them, then out He goes. We will trust God so long as He lets us run our own show. When our own show turns out to be a flop we blame Him. All of us need to look more closely at what trust in God really means.

To begin with, trust in God is an act of total commitment. In this act of commitment let us not believe that God somehow treats us like machines, taking away our will and removing our personality. The baby in the home is committed to the care of the parents. The child does not know it but certainly trusts his parents. Because this element of commitment is present in the life of the child, it does not mean that the child's will or the child's appetite or the child's personality is taken away. As a matter of fact, the child finds ample room to exert his influence in that realm of commitment. (I am sure many a mother wishes she could exercise the same control over her baby as she can over the radio or TV!) No you are not less a man or a woman, you are more, when you trust God with your life.

The self in me always leads me up blind alleys and puts me in the place where I can trust no one. It is much like the owner of a factory who hired a night watchman and every night went down to his factory to watch the night watchman; or the housewife whose physician suggested she get someone in twice a week to do her housework so she could get out and find some relaxation — she got someone in but stayed home to supervise her. It is this transfer of self to God, where we can put our confidence in Him, that brings reality to Christian living and boundless assurance to our lives.

But trust in God does not remove the hazards of this life. We need to know that God has placed us all in His school. In His school we are to learn many lessons. Right at the top of the blackboard are the words for all to see, "Here we have no continuing city." God puts us in His school knowing full well that ignorance, folly and sin would cause us suffering. Do you think that parents who have to employ some discipline to keep a child in school are motivated by hate? Like the child we sometimes tell God that we do not want to go to school. We want to be happy and carefree. We just do not want the mental strain that school imposes.

If we are to understand the meaning of trust in God we must drop the idea that trust means sunny days, moonlit nights and much self-indulgence. Trust in God does not remove the hazards of this life, but it does offer courage and faith to face them.

> With the shade and with the sunshine,
> With the joy and with the pain,
> Lord, I trust thee, both are needed
> Me, the wayward child to train.
> Earthly loss, did we but know it
> Often means our heavenly gain.

This is the Gospel that Jesus came to preach.

OUR REFORMATION HERITAGE

Therefore being justified by faith, we have peace with God through our Lord, Jesus Christ. ROMANS 5:1

The greatest foe a man can know is the foe that lurks within the camp. Our greatest perplexities today come from the things internal and not from the things external. No life can be safe while the Devil is enthroned in the heart. No family can be happy while a renegade clings to its altar. No society can be immune while a traitor crouches at the door. No organization can proclaim its worth until its members live and breathe the atmosphere of its standards and seek to live out the principles on which it rests. No creed can serve its purpose unless its veins are kept open with the pure blood of deep conviction. An open Bible is of no value unless its holy precepts are observed and its Divine challenge made a living reality.

What then is our Reformation legacy? It was just for such principles that our Protestant Reformation came into being, not by chance, but by Divine imposition. From Germany, its birthplace, it spread establishing itself with firmer roots in Switzerland through Zwingli and Calvin. It awakened Denmark and Holland to a new life. It came to England and Scotland through Latimer and Knox. It gave birth to Presbyterianism in Scotland and transformed the British nation through Cromwell, Milton and Bunyon. It brought into existence the great American Republic. It has, in these past four hundred years, gone into all parts of the world with its positive evangel and has faced privation and death in order to make Christ known, in a personal way, to a sinful humanity.

More than that, Protestantism made possible the conditions in which our modern discoveries of science, our progress in commerce, art and education were borne. Lest we forget, in a world of so much confusion, I would remind you that wherever Protestantism is the religion of the country, there you will find liberty and freedom. There you will recognize truth and justice as the chief characteristics of its political life.

Protestantism is still the world's greatest need. As we look over the world today we are made aware that a grave departure from Protestant principles has taken place. Think, if you will, of the extravagant nationalism that has asserted itself today throughout the world. The danger in rabid nationalism is simply that it claims complete submission over its subjects. It is above Christ, above the Church, above the family, above the individual and indeed claims to be above right or wrong.

It has always been proclaimed from the house tops that Protestantism is inseparably wedded to free institutions, to free press, to freedom of thought, to freedom of action and it gives to all equal liberty and security. We must keep in mind, lest we be interpreted incorrectly, that Protestantism is a spiritual force and true Protestantism cannot be separated from its foundation, the Bible, which is its rule of faith and practice, the inspiration of its political aspirations and the guide for all its actions. It must be kept to the fore. Having built itself up on the Everlasting Rock of Holy Scripture, it stands secure against paganism and political storms.

Protestantism knows no middle way in its proclamation of truth or in its denunciation of error. It realizes that a neutral course is not competent to deal rightly with the foe so it calls today, as it did in days gone by, to attack the enemy's position in a clear-cut and positive way. The Protestant Church today must stand in the stream of her heritage and declare, in a simple and yet abiding faith, her faith in Jesus Christ who is Lord of all. There is the necessity to post, as Luther did, the ninety-five thesis on the enemy door. To say with him, "I will go to the Diet, though every tile on the housetop were a Devil." Stand by him and declare, "Here I stand! I can do naught else, God helping me."

Let me assure you that this is not the easy way. The roadway of righteousness is not the pleasant path that some make it out to be. There are sacrifices to be made, battles to fight and oppressions to bear. It is true to say that the days of fiendish persecution have passed. We shall never be called to die at the stake for our faith. We shall never be required to ride to death in chariots of fire, or sit on red hot irons, or stand the pain of the thumbscrew, or perish in the incoming tide. No one will behead us if we respond to the challenge of Christ and follow Him faithfully. Our fathers and mothers of the Reformation gladly endured all that, rather than surrender principle and disown allegiance to the Master.

While that day is gone, and I pray God forever, it has been followed by another that makes it harder for a Protestant to be a Protestant. Let a man have personal convictions about his faith today, in private or in public, and let him make them known and he will have a great price to pay. There will be a circle of society from which he will be completely excluded. There will be public and private offices that will shut their doors in his face. There will be a reproach to bear, a cross to carry, a rough road to travel, if we fall in line with our Protestant principles and make them the standard of our life and conduct.

It is along such a roadway that Protestantism takes its direction. It is a roadway of conflict, battle and strife, and yet Protestantism is seen at its best, under fire. It was borne in conflict but in that conflict she has produced her greatest saints and her masters of art and statesmanship. In a day when the tendency is to belittle our faith and heritage and to depict Protestantism as just another religion among many others, it is well and just to pause and let the world know that Protestantism is the greatest power that has ever come into our world. It has been the dynamic of every worthy attainment and the only hope for the peace, security and prosperity of our world. It has brightened and bettered every life and land it has ever touched in education, happiness, purity and goodwill. As such, we need not fear to be a part of it and to make a true witness of it to the world.

The challenge, as I see it today, is to recapture, as the Reformers did, the reality of Jesus and His relationship to God, His Church and mankind. Jesus, in our faith, is seen as the Saviour of men. This should be underlined when we think about the purpose and the work of His Church in the world. The Lordship of Christ is the one thing that will continue to destroy all the attempts of men, whether it be in the Church or in the state, to set up intermediaries to take His place.

The Reformer knew that man could only find his true life in Jesus Christ, for Christ was God's Man to reconcile the world unto Himself. That is why the apostle declared, "Therefore being justified by faith, we have peace with God through our Lord, Jesus Christ."

This surely is the foundation upon which the Reformed Church rests. We must not accept anything less nor must we add or take away from this great thought. If there is one weakness in our faith today it is the lack of centrality of Christ in the Church, in our worship and in our Christian witness. We must re-examine our faith in the light of all these truths, allowing Christ to be our Saviour, guide and friend.

LEADERSHIP

In considering the concept of leadership, we are addressing one of the most vital aspects of any organization. Behind every movement there is a leader and without leadership no movement can survive. It is true that the movement is always bigger than the leader or the institution, but by the same token, nothing worthwhile occurs in our world without being first initiated by an aggressive leader.

In every field of human endeavour the most important commodity is still the leader and the leader's personality. No one needs to be a specialist to be a good leader. A leader does not need to be a superman, does not need to possess many rare gifts, does not need to be versatile in every field of endeavour, does not even need to be a highly educated man or woman. What a leader most needs is to know where he is going, to use what gifts he has to get there, to be loyal, to be understood, to have vision, to give time and preparation to his cause. Success is not something acquired — it is something that is achieved through hard work and effort. A leader must have a deep sense of discipline, possess resourcefulness and have boundless initiative.

To advance any cause, a leader must know the meaning of discipline. It is not enough to seek discipline for others. We must have it in abundance ourselves. He cannot lead who does not see the way. The cause always demands that a leader be resourceful. That is to say he must be able to find ways and means to keep his cause alive. He must have more than one road along which he can go if he is to find the necessary material to give life and blood to his convictions. In the field of initiative the leader is challenged simply because every good cause requires the initiative of some person.

No one can be a leader unless he has followers and no cause can live unless it has people to support it. Hence, the leader must allow himself the right to interpret for those that follow. This does not mean, of course, that he will not co-operate but he will use in that co-operation, the genius of personal initiative to get out of people the thing which he believes is best for the cause. Followers bring with them their own peculiar traits. Here, the leader is confronted with a mixture of personalities which will require that he must have his wits about him at all times.

To work is an integral part of the leader's responsibility. Where work is not accomplished it may simply be the result of not having the right kind of leaders. It is the responsibility of the leader to be prepared for every eventuality, and where this is not done, we stumble along because we have not given ourselves a chance.

Good leadership embodies many characteristics. Be enthusiastic making what you do real; love what you do and do what you love; be a big-hearted person; love people not for their faults but for their possibilities; shun negativism; be constructive and helpful making the best of what you have; build up your leadership by helpful habits; be courteous, punctual, loyal, presentable, informative; and most importantly, be sincere.

REMEMBRANCE

There are some things that we can never forget. There are happenings in our lives that only death will erase from our memories. You will never forget your wedding day. Where is the parent who will forget the holy joy of the first born? Show me the mother who has stood in the cold and lonely corridor of a hospital ward while all that she loves is on the operating table. Minutes are hours and every footstep in her direction, a horrible nightmare. When the surgeon appears does he need to speak to let her know that he is the messenger of good news? This mother, to her dying day, will never forget the words, "Out of danger." There are countless joys and tragedies in life that we will never forget.

Who among us, old enough to understand, will forget May 1945. Across our world was flashed the words of victory. Hostilities had ceased. The enemy was defeated and another world conflict had come to an end. War had produced an aching void in the heart that this world could never repair and a longing in the soul that could never be silenced until the day would break and the shadows flee away. While death is the most familiar incident in life, it is always cruel and hard to understand. The poet expresses it best when he says:

Here dead we lie, because we did not choose to live,
And spurn the land from which we sprung.
Life to be sure is nothing much to lose,
But young men think it so, and we were young.

War had brought death and with its coming, intimate fellow-ships were broken, fond dreams perished and well built castles of promise had been shattered. With victory, the nightmare of uncertainty had vanished. The fear that gripped your heart whenever you saw the telegraph boy on your street — and you had seen him there so often — was gone. Around your knees you gathered your little flock and with a heart overflowing with the joy of certainty, you could begin, at last, to make preparations for an important homecoming. You will always remember that too.

We must never forget the brave men, and there were so many of them, who went to war and did not return. We live because they died. In the ministry of human sacrifice we are always made conscious of the fact that our survival is due to the willing heart that shares our load and dies our death. This land of freedom with its free institutions, governments, halls of learning; its free and unscarred homes and open houses of worship, has not come merely by chance or thrift, it has come by the way our comrades chose — the way of sacrifice. Across the world they stood against the tyrant's wicked hand and gave their all to save us from a ruthless slavery. Their broken bodies did not hide, in death, the counte-nance of an unbroken faith. They believed, as we must believe, that the way to a better world is along the pathway of personal sacrifice. As long as we continue to produce such men and women so long will our land live.

If they died that we might live, then we must so live that their sacrifice has not been in vain. We are always in danger of accepting too easily and too casually, our common debt to freedom. We are only free as long as we are ready to protect our freedom. Freedom is the fruit of "toil, sweat and tears". The military strength of a nation is no guarantee of freedom. A victory won upon a battlefield is no surety of freedom. Freedom can only be main-tained when the minds of men are free.

Peace must be our objective, to build aright upon the gallant sacrifice of our dead heroes. These are important truths we must remember. The one thing that now disturbs us is the ugly fact that victory did not, nor does not, mean peace. Victory, in every age, has only been a geographical term. We defeat the enemy in the west only to find him better prepared and more destructive in the east. He wars again who only has been defeated by man. Victory by men over men, is only a temporary thing. There does not appear to be anything in this world that man, through personal intelligence, or scientific method can make permanent or abiding. If this be so can we ever hope for peace in the world?

Peace can be a reality if pursued through the proper channels. All approaches to peace today are made on human levels. There is abroad, the feeling that peace can come through the wise legislative policies of statesmen. I believe that everything these men do is all to the good; however, unless we can come with them to the realization that war is sin, we cannot find in manmade measures, an effective remedy for war. It appears that nations are now measuring their security in terms of a monopoly on atomic power. This is not the answer. Temporary terms with peace is not the solution. The permanent and not the transient should be our goal.

Peace must be a spiritual venture to be abiding. Only as men and nations come to the Cross of Christ and learn of Him, the love that casts out hate, can we ever hope to rid our world of war. The darkness in our world today can only be dissolved in the victorious light that shines from the Cross.

Let our prayers be that men and nations will turn to Him and turning, find the peace that is eternal.

THE WAY TO PERMANENT PEACE

God the Lord will speak peace unto His people, and to His saints, but let them not turn again to folly. PSALM 85:8

The restoration of Israel from exile is proof that God had forgiven His people and had taken them back into His favour as He promised. Yet the present condition of Israel seems to show that

God's anger still rests upon them. Disappointment and disaster are crushing them. The national life has not been revived. The great hopes held out by the prophets, in conjunction with their return, has not been realized and thus the nation prays for a fresh manifestation of God's saving power to gladden His people.

The Psalmist received the assurance that God's purposes of good toward His faithful people will surely be fulfilled. He will dwell among them and bless them, fulfilling the prophetic promises of the establishment of His Kingdom among men.

The Psalm was written to address the depression and the despondency which were rapidly crushing the feeble church of the restoration. It delivers the assurance that the prophetic promises of a glorious Messianic future were not a delusion but that God would establish His Kingdom in His land. The Psalm is full of Messianic hope, finding its ultimate fulfillment in Christ.

I believe this Psalm has significance to a modern society. As you read it you cannot help but be struck by the modern condition that it reveals. Think for a moment of the days that darkened our world when war devastated nations taking from them the finest manhood and womanhood, and bringing the nations of the world together in one of the bloodiest conflicts ever witnessed by history. Our hearts go out this day to all who will continue to suffer from that experience. Many are the homes that grew up fatherless. Many are the children who were born with a father overseas who never had the privilege of seeing him in the flesh. There are thousands of mothers who have been deprived of their sons and who sit this day still mourning their loss. Today we come to acknowledge the heroism of our men and women and to thank God for giving us such splendid and courageous individuals. Our prayers can only be that God will continue to endow our nation with the same lofty courage, the same spirit of sacrifice, the same noble willingness and the same great devotion.

Today we find a generation that knows nothing of the tragic results of world conflict. Many have said that this was a war to end wars and have worked hard to make that hope a living reality. I am not so sure, however, that we are moving in the right direction. I am not so sure that we have laid the necessary foundation for such a hope. I am not so sure that we have been implementing the right initiatives to obtain the great peace of the world.

I believe that the nations are placing too much confidence

in themselves and too little in God. Like the people of old, we have allowed the prosperity of a few years to shut God off from our lives. We have built to ourselves our own gods and have begun to worship them. In the mad rush of selfish ambition many have lost their souls. We have failed to take God into our calculations. If permanent peace is to come to this world of ours, we must come first of all to the source of peace. Like the people of old, we must learn that the restoration of peace comes from God.

Peace can only come when God has made His peace to reign in the heart of man. The individual heart must be touched by the heart of God. I have a belief that the success of any nation depends largely upon the individual effort that is put forth. It has been a common failure of civilization that all its work, all its thinking, all its constructive or destructive manipulation has been confined to a few individuals. If every individual had a rightful say then things might be different. I am convinced that the starting point for peace lies with each individual. While he must clamour for the external reconstruction of the affairs of the nation and of industry, he must also be prepared to look in upon his own heart and see if a change needs to take place there. Possibly he will find space for reconstruction in his own life. If his conduct is set in the right direction then he will be able to go forth and set up a better world, opening the doors for the coming in of peace.

This can only be accomplished when men come to acknowledge a greater power in their lives than their own. God must be made the controlling force in the life of man before He can become the controlling force in the life of the nation. When the hearts of men have been saved by Christ, the heart of the nation is also saved. This must be our starting place. It behooves you and me to be in the peace of God. We must recognize that He is the only power that is able to break down the walls of indifference and to set the world free from the Beast of War.

We need to examine the challenge of peace to the people of God. What have we as Christians done for the cause of peace? Has the Church of God come forward with all its power to attack the enemies of peace? Has the Church sought any spiritual affront to see that it is maintained?

I am afraid, in this arena, we have never made a move nor have we shown any bold stand for its cause. It is true that some formal efforts have been made, but they show themselves to be lifeless and ineffective. The man on the street never took less notice of organized religion than he does today. Many churches have fallen asleep to their great spiritual responsibility and in some measure have lost the unique ideal of Christ. There seems to be no life in us when issues of importance come to the fore. We seem to have no men and women ready to stand and contend for the noble truth, as it is to be found in Jesus. At a time like this, when our world is calling for peace, what are we doing as individuals or as a Church to make it a reality?

Some will tell us that it is not the business of the Church to bother with matters of a political nature. Whoever said that peace was confined to the realm of politics? Frankly, politicians have had too much to do with it and they have failed. They have been moving in the wrong direction. They have not centred their power in God. They have not invested themselves with the garment of righteousness. They have failed to bring Christ into consideration.

It is up to the Christian and the Christian Church to show the banner of Christ for the great cause of peace. It is our common lot and our deep and abiding responsibility, to start thinking in terms of peace and allow Christ to have a say in the affairs of the world. We have not been displaying the courage that belongs to the Christian religion. We have not been showing all the fortitude that is to be found in Christ. We have not been utilizing our powers of faith or our holy insight.

There is a great need to recharge our religion with spiritual power. There is a great longing to put into practice the simple teachings of Christ. I have a feeling that the days for more consecration of life are at hand. The hour for undivided service to our Master has arrived at our doorstep.

We can never hope to get the results that we should, unless we choose the Christ-way and the Christ-spirit. I call upon all church members to arise, for the hour of living service is at hand. The moment for striking has come and the days of our sleeping have passed.

As I see it there has been too much coddling of the saints within the Church and too little effort in the direction of saving sinners. Conventions, retreats, prophetic conferences may continue until Judgment Day and be very much enjoyed by those who patronize them. Unless they result in increased devotion to Jesus and His great saving purpose; unless the outcome results in more wholehearted and unselfish service in seeking and saving the lost, their value is questionable.

As the church edifice is built brick by brick or stone by stone so the Spiritual Kingdom is built by individual men and women, saved and won, by the constraining level of Jesus Christ, from unrighteousness to purity, goodness and peace.

Give your all then, as Christ did, for the coming peace of the world. His peace is that which lasts and abides forever. May God in the name of Christ make it so and use us as the instruments to bring it about.

THE CONSOLATION OF RELIGION

I will never leave thee, nor forsake thee. HEBREWS 13:5

One of the difficult problems we have to face is the problem of being able to relate our faith to the many disturbing happenings in our world.

There are times when we presume to speak for God while in reality we are speaking from our own limited experience. Many of us are like the dear old lady who lived in the backwoods all her life. On coming to the city and observing the cars, subways, noise and rush, she exclaimed, "God sure has made a mess of things here." She, too, was speaking out of a very limited experience. Reflect upon the city dweller who had never been to the country in his life. He arrived at his uncle's farm at milking time and was instructed to go to the barn where he would find his uncle. There on a stool sat his uncle, a pail between his knees, milking a cow. After taking in the scene and reflecting upon it for some few minutes, he looked at his uncle and then at the calm face of the cow and said, "God sure has made things awkward for you up here." He, too, was speaking out of a limited experience.

I sometimes think we treat God like the military police treated the troops . . . they were always putting up signs that read *Out of Bounds.*

We have got to think of God and His plan for our life as that which cannot be pegged down or bounded by restrictions. Our God is boundless. Our God is infinite. If you want to know about Him you should read what He has to say in His book. We need to stop taking our ideas about God from novels, from magazine writers, from radio scribes who only gossip about Him. We need to go to the Bible, read it and let it speak to us. Its message is for you. It is the message that your heart can understand.

Nothing happens in your life or mine, whether it be joy or sorrow, pain or pleasure, failure or success, but your Heavenly Father is beside you.

I will never leave thee, nor forsake thee.

That is His promise and upon that you should build your hope. This does not mean that because He is near we will always avoid disaster or despair. In this life we learn some very hard lessons and we learn them in fear, frustration and tears. But in spite of that, we can be sure that we are in His hands and nothing can surprise Him.

I often get letters, phone calls and visits where the conversation begins something like this: "You'll be surprised to hear . . . that Bill has begun drinking again, . . . that Mary has left her husband, . . . that Albert is in jail, . . . that Henry has run away from home. I may be surprised but we can't surprise God. On the other hand, there are many pleasant surprises. Perhaps we do not speak about them enough. Is it not a pleasant surprise when someone who has closed his life and his heart to God, suddenly opens the door and lets Him in? Is it not a pleasant surprise when someone who was regarded as a thief has become honest and is willing to discharge his debt? When family relationships have broken down, is it not a pleasant surprise to discover that the cord of love has been mended? Is it not a pleasant surprise when that do-nothing on your street or in your community becomes a useful member of society? It may all surprise us but we cannot surprise God.

I suppose the darkest hour in history was when the Cross raised its ugly head and bore our Lord to His death. There were those who rubbed their hands with glee but we know now, and are not surprised to learn, that the Cross was only the dark background to a living and abiding love,

My sinful self, my only shame,
My glory all, the cross.

If God can do that with the Cross what might He do with the evil in our lives. If so dark a deed as this was not beyond His power of transformation, will He be beaten by war, by hate, by the personal problems of your little life and mine?

There are certainly conditions that make it all possible. God cannot work His Divine healing in a heart that harbours a grudge. There are people and families who suffer a crushing bereavement and have never come to terms with it in their own hearts. They cannot summon their loved one from the dead, yet there is a lurking bitterness inside them. They envy the happiness of others and speak sourly of the good health which rogues appear to enjoy. In their heart they are up-in-arms against God. There are people who may have suffered a shattered romance or a lost fortune, or some bodily malformation, or some serious injury, or terrible accident — something they endure because they must but which they never willingly accept and that grudge remains a hindrance to the power of God.

I once knew a man who held a grudge against the Church for years because someone else was appointed over him to a church office. I knew another lady who told me she would leave this church if she had to sit beside a man who, in her mind, did not know how to conduct himself during a service. What she didn't know was that this man had spent many years of his life in our reformatories and just two weeks previously in my office he had opened the door of his black and dejected heart to Christ. I had encouraged him to come to church.

These are the things in life that dam the stream of God's mercy. Resignation to the hurts of life is not enough. We must have reconciliation with Christ. Stopping at the bridge of your difficulties is resignation. Going over, in faith, is reconciliation.

You remember when Paul was imprisoned by Nero. He did not rail at God or Nero. He transformed his prison by calling himself a prisoner of Jesus Christ. When Dr. Bardarno lost his lovely little son at nine years of age, to diphtheria, he did not accuse heaven and protest to the Almighty he said, "This loss has only intensified my desire to continue . . . the work of child rescue . . . I could but resolve afresh, as I then did, that by God's grace I would consecrate myself to the task of rescuing helpless little ones from the miseries of a neglected and sinful life . . . I dare not turn aside from this work." The same could be said of John Howard and Elizabeth Fry.

If you carry a grudge surrender it to Him. That is the only way to find the peace of God. Trust Him, Love Him, Follow Him, Obey Him.

SPIRIT-FILLED LIVES

For I am determined not to know anything among you, save Jesus Christ, and Him crucified. I CORINTHIANS 2:2

Our text provides the needed conviction and expression of Christianity today. It is not to be taken, however, as the words of one, who because of his ignorance, could only so declare himself. To the contrary, if we know the life, mind and high intellectual attainments of Paul we can well say that it was not because he was ignorant of the worldly pursuits of men but rather he wanted to ignore them in order that he might attain the true object of his faith.

He lived in a world of much self-glorification, self-assertion and self-expression. He knew what it was to value one's own claims and one's own convictions. For years he had been a slave to his own intellectual desires and he knew, too, how to deal with those who opposed the prevailing thought of the day. In the death of Stephen we get a clear picture of what it meant to be an apostle of something other than that which was the accepted religion and thought of the day.

Paul was mindful of this. He realized just how far such knowledge could lead one and how destructive it was to obtaining a higher and better life. He knew himself to be a rigid champion of formalism and a strict task master where punishment had to be handed out to any offenders. In all this there was futility and failure. There was nothing to charge the soul with new life. Nothing to lift the ban of sin or to set the conscience free. Guilt and despair were the total gains from living such a life.

It is no wonder then, that Paul comes before the people of Corinth with this great exclamation and affirmation of his faith. If they were looking for worldly wisdom or worldly testimony they would be disappointed. Paul comes with but one message and that message concerns the Christ. It is not Paul, the great philosopher. It is not Paul, the great debater. It is not Paul, the great rational reasoner. It is a man whose life has been permeated with the love of Christ. A man who has learned the seeming uselessness of one's own human endeavours. What Paul actually does here, is to relinquish his hold on his own powers by throwing himself wholly at the disposal of Christ. Paul says, in effect, "I have nothing to tell except that which I have received from Christ. I have no message of my own. What I have to say concerns my Lord and my Saviour."

In taking this stand he is naturally inviting trouble and dispute. He is not here to argue about his faith. He is not even discussing it. He knows what he has to say cannot be argued. He knows that the faith, that is his, is to be accepted and not discussed. "I am on a mission in which I am only the instrument. It is Christ speaking through me."

It is not Paul, that he wants men to hear or to acknowledge, but it is Paul's Christ. Nothing will shift him from that position. Nothing will mar that conviction. There is nothing to take the place of such a faith.

I believe what Paul is seeking to do, is the very thing that is most needed in our present day Christianity. I am aware that such a stand today may seem dogmatic. To the men and women who feel the very burning presence of Christ in life, only such a stand is possible. A positive acknowledgement of Christ produces a healthy faith. It is faith that will make us speak the message and heart of Christ. Is it not true that we are seeking to reach people by other means and other devices? If only we could learn the heart of our text, what a blessed boon it would be to the Church and to the world.

I feel certain that one of the first things that such an experience would achieve, is to take out of our religion much of its falsity and self-righteousness. We have a tendency to feel that we are indispensable to Christianity. Most of us who feel that way are guilty of not knowing what Christianity really is. When Christ comes into a heart and that heart bends to His holy and just will, that is the very time that we feel our utter helplessness. The men and women that speak in the language of Paul are usually the men and women who feel that they are the greatest of sinners.

The Christ-moved life is the life that ever feels its incompleteness. It is never satisfied with its own attainments. It is so conscious of its own failing and sin that it finds it is necessary to live in a very close companionship with Christ. It is this feeling of our own worth that is greatly hindering the spiritual advancement of the Church of Christ. When we know ourselves to be nothing then we become faithful evangels of the Gospel.

What then has our text to teach? "I know nothing save Christ, and Him crucified." It reminds us, in the first instance, that the successful Christian life is spirit-moved. This is an extremely important concept. There is not enough emphasis placed upon the Holy Spirit in relation to Christian life. We need to know that the Spirit of Christ is the power to life. If you are finding your Christian life shallow and unattractive; if you are finding your Christian work a piece of hard labour, if you at times, feel like giving it up, the blame can well be traced to the inactivity of the Spirit of God in your life. If you find that your prayers do not take on meaning and will not take the shape of words, you can well attribute such a condition to the lack of the Spirit of God in your life. The Spirit of God cannot work where there is no freedom for Him to have His way.

But when you lay yourself at its disposal as did Paul, you will find that your life will be enriched and overflowing with thanksgiving to God. If you are finding that your life is not producing to the honour and glory of God, I think you will see that you are simply not allowing His Spirit to govern and instill the thought of heaven in your heart. We famish our souls unless we open them to God's Spirit.

Paul was only able to speak as he did because the Spirit of God had possessed him. When we are Spirit-possessed we will begin to sing a new song. The hard and difficult places and tasks will take on new meaning. What seemed dead to us will become alive, when His Spirit shines in our hearts.

We can never speak with assurance as did Paul. We can never speak with conviction until we know that it is in the power and glory of the Spirit that we proclaim our message.

This Spirit-filled life is our greatest need because our work in this place is not equal to our own powers. Nothing of vital importance can be done for the Kingdom until we submit to the way of the Spirit. I wonder how many of us are trusting to the Spirit to make known the will of God in our lives. I wonder how many of us are relying upon His power to give us victory over our sin and our human weaknesses. We are sure to remain stumbling blocks to the cause that we represent, unless our lives ring true and clear with a glowing anthem of the Spirit of God.

The reason that most people refuse to allow His Spirit to work is because He confronts us with our sin and calls continually for our surrender. He breaks us where we feel that we can afford to be broken. He strips us where we feel that we can be revealed. He shows us in a true light, not only before God, but to the world. This is more than we are ready for. He never leaves us until He has won the victory for God.

Is this not the kind of Christianity that we want? Is this not the kind of power that we need to make us the faithful witnesses that God would have us be? I pray that to the Spirit of God we may yield today; that to His way we may come with penitent hearts; that to His power we may resign. All this we need in the Church. All this we need in our lives. All this we need if we are going to be more than conquerors.

May His Spirit be yours now and may we say with Paul, "I am determined to know nothing among you save Christ and Him crucified."

THE BIBLE AND ITS MESSAGE

There is nothing that raises the mind or the affections to the highest level as a right relationship with God. When we obtain a right relationship between God and our hearts, we gradually attain, in ourselves, a true and honest note. We begin to learn the worth of our moral being. It is only then that we comprehend the great truth that life has an end which makes it worth living. It is the Bible alone that gives such hope to man and without these great truths to feed our souls, life would be exceedingly poor and meaningless.

It is the Bible that gives us the true knowledge of God. When we look at the ancient world and seek for an idea of God it presents us with a spectacle of ignorance. In one place, it is the sun, moon and planets that are the object of worship. Elsewhere, temples are built to four-footed beasts and creeping things of the earth. In other places the great natural objects — the sky, the dawn, the rivers, the rain and the fire — are the favourite deities. In Greece and Rome men adored gods sculptured in forms of human beauty. These religions clung to a myriad of superstitions. Many of the rites were licentious and revolting. Where, in all of these practices could man get one idea to elevate him, one impulse to raise him above himself to nobler deeds. In Britain when the light of Christianity first broke upon it, Druid priests chanted their mysterious songs and carried out their mystic ceremonies in dim forest recesses. The tribes, who supplanted them brought their traditions. They sang the praises of Thor and Oden and revelled in the prospect of Valhalla where they would drink blood from the skulls of their slain enemies. From time to time, Christianity has risen up and cast aside the worst of these corruptions. In every case it is the Bible that has been the instrument of God's Spirit, causing these reformations. It has been the Bible, which has been the agency in that long series of historical revivals, by which the Church has once and again been saved in the days of stagnation and unbelief. Without the Bible not one of these great changes would have taken place. It is the knowledge of God, as revealed in the Bible, that has produced the brightest and best in civilization.

What then are the results of this knowledge of God as it is set forth in the Bible? In the first place it is because of the Gospel of Jesus Christ that we today are not worshipping stones and idols, but rather are bowing in acknowledgement to the one God and Father of our Lord Jesus Christ who is above all and in all. In the early centuries, it was Christianity that overthrew the reign of the gods and goddesses of Greece and Rome and swept them into oblivion. No one today so much as dreams of the possibility of their revival. It was Christianity that laid hold of the rough Barbarian peoples who overran Europe, and trained them and molded them into a civilized society. It was Christianity in Scotland that set forth a light in the monasteries of Iona and by and by spread its beams through every part of the country. It is Christianity today that is teaching the idolaters to burn their idols, to worship the true God and to take upon themselves the obligations of a decent and civilized existence.

There are also the personal blessings of the Gospel that the Bible has brought to us. Think of our many churches it has built; our Sabbath deliberations; our religion that inspires so much earnest living and so much noble work; the blessed effect of that religion in peace, in strength, in moral impulse, in the minds that possess it; the comfort that it dispenses in trial; the joy and triumph that it gives in death — all this is the fruit of the Bible.

Some will ask, "If that be the message and work of the Bible, why is the world in the condition that we find it today?" Frankly, the redemptive work of the Bible is not yet complete. Christ's reign is not yet ended. It will endure until the Divine plan is completed. At the same time, I feel that we must stop blaming God for the condition of the world and commence looking inward upon ourselves. The world will continue to be as it is until we start working with God. Most of the world's problems today, can be traced to the fact that man has been leaving God outside his own plans. The God-way must be chosen if we are to see a brighter and better world. His way is not the easy way. It is not the way, in worldly terms, that receives all the gain and all the wealth, but it is the way that leads to life eternal and to a life in this world that is able to endure and face the worst kind of opposition and emerge victorious.

The reason that God's way, for so many, seems dark and uncertain is simply because they have refused to use the light of God to shine before them. God's light to us is His own Holy Word, and not until we find ourselves searching it out and living by its holy teaching will we ever enjoy the life and light that comes from Him. To seek to lead a Christian life without a thorough knowledge of the Bible, is like asking a captain of a boat to start out upon his journey without a compass. To disregard the Bible in our lives means that we will go far astray. Many fall by the wayside because they have been careless in their reading and studying of the Bible.

One needs only to observe a Christian congregation to notice how careless we are regarding the Bible and its use. How many today carry their Bibles to the House of God? I remember being at a church and calling for a responsive reading. We couldn't carry it out because no one thought to bring their Bibles along.

Let us return to our Bibles and allow its truths to speak to us. It can do more for us than all the preaching, all the teaching, all the organized Christian work that is now in existence. It will help us to understand what God has to say and what He expects of those who claim to be His children.

I have a feeling that much of the dissatisfaction that is present today in the Church would quickly disappear if the members of the Church knew their Bible. Even the sermons, the hymns, the prayers and all the rest would be better understood and would provide a greater blessing if we came to the House of God with the love of the Bible in our hearts.

In summary let me suggest that you go home today, choose a passage, read it and re-read it. Try to see what God is saying to you. Take time for prayer, take time for God to speak to you; take time to study it, use every occasion to test the word. Above all else, be loyal to its demands and be faithful in carrying them out.

There is no greater weapon we can use to make our attack upon the sin, sham, selfishness, greed and moral laxity of our day than the Bible. There is no solution that the world needs more to solve its many problems than the Word of God.

Let me ask you to be proclaimers of the message of the Bible and allow it to function faithfully, reverently, sincerely in your lives. The results of the past are sure to be the results of the future. The Bible remains the spiritual hope of the world. It holds the power for every worthy enterprise. God grant that He may use us to be the servants of righteousness that His will may be carried out in us for the salvation of the world.

THIS IS MY FAITH

*And Jesus said, No man, having put his hand to the plough,
and looking back, is fit for the Kingdom of God.* LUKE 9:62

The faith that is mine, in a very real sense, is not mine at all. I did not earn it. I did not buy it. It was given to me. It came by the grace of Him who is my Lord and Saviour. No one can really speak of his conversion. We must learn to speak of His Redemption. Neither can I truly speak of my ministry, I must learn to speak of His ministry. Whatever has happened here is not because of anything we have done, but has happened because of the great things He has been pleased to do in our lives and church. There is no such thing as an isolated Christian. No one comes to his spiritual decisions alone.

I was fortunate to be reared in the atmosphere of a Christian home and at no time can I remember ever being outside the reach of Christian communication. The home, the Church, Christian friends and ministers, teachers, all had a share in preparing me for the faith that is mine. It is not what happens at one's conversion that is important so much as that which happens afterwards.

I was to learn in my days as a student minister, that there are many disappointments to face when working with men and women. Even where one would expect agreement on Christian things it does not always exist. The Church, the body of our Lord, appears to have many inconsistent members, who by their conduct, render a disservice to the Church of Christ. I was soon to learn that I was not sent to judge but to preach. It was not my place to fit everyone into my own mold. My task was to be loyal to the Church and obedient to her Lord. When I did not find things as I thought they should be, I shouldn't run away and look for like-minded people who agreed with me and who spiritually were in tune with me. I was to keep my hand on the plough. It wasn't refuge but exposure I was to seek. I was to keep my feet in the furrow and my eyes on Him.

If God is going to do anything with us He has to have people who will "stick and not jump". Candidly, we have too many "jumpers" in the Church today. I remember early in my ministry, a family who were always telling me about the good sermons they heard at other churches. Yet when we had a bit of ploughing to do here they were never around. They always wanted to be in on the harvest but not the ploughing.

The real and vital work of this church has been accomplished by men and women, young and old, who, while they could have enjoyed a more radiant ministry, a more comfortable place to worship, a less sacrificial service, nonetheless put their hand to the plough refusing to turn back. When they accepted the vows of membership, "Do you promise to maintain and support the work of this church?", they kept their vows and stuck to their Christian task.

When I was ordained here in 1935, I presented the standards of our faith to the little group and together, for I have never asked anyone to accept anything that I do not practice myself, we laid the foundation of Christian stewardship and pledged ourselves to give our time, our talents and our treasury to the Lord. When you get that the Lord gets a "sticker".

Out of that conviction miracles began to happen. First, we bought this site. Next, we put up our church basement. Our congregation began to grow. The church, that under our system couldn't be, was now taking hold. We were becoming an example to others right across this country. I remember a letter from a ladies' auxiliary in one of our churches who wrote making enquiries, "If we don't have bazaars and bake sales the minister will not get his salary." I was told the same thing here in the early days but I can tell you today that I have never missed my salary. As a matter of fact, it is always in my hand ahead of time.

O, Foolish Galatians who hath bewitched thee.

When the whole man — his time, talents and treasury — are in the control of Christ you can accomplish whatever you set out to do. You can bring happiness to your life and purpose to your church. On every side we are told it cannot be done. Of course it cannot, unless Christ is in your life and in your church. If you are here today and have any doubts about the value of committed life, just have a look around at the church, the youth centre, the men and women who sit in this sanctuary who made it so. You cannot do these things on an eight hour shift nor can you do them without dedicated men and women.

Will you put your hand on the plough? Will you let Christ direct the furrows of your life? Will you, this Lord's Day, give yourself to Him? I can recommend His way as the only way. Young people put your life at His disposal and even greater things will happen in this place. The work is not complete. It is yours to do and carry on. Your fathers have laid the foundation so in His name, build.

CHRISTMAS

And when they were come into the house. MATTHEW 2:11

It is hard for anyone to say anything new about Christmas. The sacred story and all its varied details has been ours ever since we were little children. It has been told so often and so well that it is difficult to conceive of a thought that has yet to be emphasized in a word, song or a picture. Yet, everytime the Biblical narrative is repeated, it reaches us with a freshness that is unique and sublime. There was something about that first Christmas morn that refuses to grow old or die. The more we try to fathom it the more we are convinced that it is something peculiarly Divine.

"And when they were come into the house, they saw the young child with Mary, his mother, and fell down and worshipped him."

The wise men who hastened for us the scenes were not wise simply because they came from the east . . . some of the wise men from the east showed themselves to be extremely foolish. Here, the wisdom implied was not just proverbial, it was rather intuitional and spiritual ... borne of holy aspirations and religious meditations. There is a pregnant lesson in that for the folk who are indifferent and indolent. Had the wise men not been waiting and watching with God, they would never have seen the beckoning star in the sky. Like many others who have been singly favoured, they might have been spared the pain of utter oblivion but they could not have reached the hallowed soil of Bethlehem.

"And when they were come into the house." What a gripping history lies behind this common phrase. One might imagine, if one knew not the background of the matter, that it was merely a mark for the end of an uneventful journey; however, the wise men had crossed a thousand perilous bridges between their homes and the homes of Nazareth. They had wild plains to cross, treacherous streams to ford and steep mountains to climb. They had keen disappointments to meet and vexing discouragements to conquer. They had the sting of reproach to bear, the jibe of mockery to withstand and the frown of contempt to face in all their miles of travel. More than one companion turned back when he saw what lay ahead. More than one pilgrim laughed at the idea of seeking the King of the Jews.

Yet the wise men were not to be baffled nor shifted from their goal. The record of their vision, heroism and success is bound up in that everyday phrase, "When they were come into the house." The lesson enforced is that ordinary things are not to be regarded in an ordinary way. There may hardly be the lifting of the voice, and in spite of that, life and death may hang on the broken syllables. One brief sentence from an earnest heart may contain a whole world of meaning. A man may come to the blessed feet of the Redeeming Lord and cry, "I surrender all", yet who can tell what struggle and self-abnegation may lie underneath that humble surrender.

Many a citizen has exercised himself patiently for the welfare of his country; many a mother has quietly denied herself for the sake of her family; many a boy and girl have sacrificed themselves secretly for the happiness of their home. Often their heroism is summed up in a few words, "When they were come into the house."

In the house what did they see? They saw the young Child with Mary, His mother. There in the lowly manger was the unspeakable gift of God. He had come from heaven to earth to seek and to save the lost. How imposing that sight must have been to all who had eyes to see. Why should God come thus, unannounced by the blare of trumpets and heralded only by a star? Why should God come thus, unattended by angels Divine and nursed only by a human hand? How glorious the deeds of a loving Father and the truthfulness of that saying that outlives the centuries, "My thoughts are not your thoughts, neither are your ways my ways." The wonder of it all would break anew upon the Magi as they saw a little babe lying in the stall wrapped in swaddling clothes.

The order of their seeing is worthy of note. They saw first the young Child, then they caught a glimpse of redeemed and honoured motherhood. It was a child and mother picture and not a picture of mother and child. The wise men were wise enough to put first things first, giving the primary place in their heart to Christ. They came into the inn that night not in response to childish whims nor to satisfy idle curiosity. They came into the inn that night not for the purpose of finding fault, not to breathe out acrid remarks. They came to the inn that night not with the intention of displaying their learning, nor with the desire to provoke bitter controversy. They came to see the promised King of Kings and Lord of All. Their mission was crowned and their hearts set rejoicing.

"They fell down and worshipped him and presented unto him, gold frankincense and myrrh." One of the great mysteries of the first Christmas morning was that so many people came into the inn and recognized not the appointed Messiah. It was not because they had yet to begin to expect Him. Prophecy long since had declared that in the fullness of time the Saviour would come and redeem the world. In the glowing light of that prophecy everyone within the favoured inn had lived and moved and had their being. Alas, the dawn of the long sought day found them so preoccupied with the treasures of the earth that they recognized not their Lord when He came knocking at their very door. They could see the young Child with His mother and some of them would say, "This is no place for a tender little infant like that." They could see the young Child with His mother and others among them would say, "God have mercy on that poor mother over there." But none of them ever guessed for a moment that in their midst the Saviour of Mankind was born. None of them ever once suspected that the Mighty God was near, waiting for the homage of their hearts. They laughed and chatted by the warmth of the fire and told, in vivid speech, of experiences by the way. Not one of them ever sensed that by their side was the King of Glory.

Such blindness by "other worldliness" has always been tragic in the realm of the soul. It is a pitiful thing that anyone should be in the presence of the Most High and never know it. Yet, that happens every Sabbath on every shore. Men and women come into the sanctuary, which is the Temple of God, and still they see everything but what they ought to see. It is simply because they give to worldy things the homage that rightly belongs to Jesus Christ. The wise men were not foolish like that. They had started out with the determination of meeting with their Lord. At every wayside inn they made it plain that they were seeking Jesus only. They had troubled all Jerusalem with the question, "Where is He that is born King of the Jews?" When they had come within the house at Bethlehem and saw the young Child with Mary His mother, they fell down and worshipped Him offering unto Him gold and frankincense and myrrh.

We too have often set out from our homes virtually crying, "Where is He that is born to be the Redeemer of my soul?" When we meet Him face to face are we ready to fall down at His feet and worship Him, offering Him the trust, devotion and service of our hearts.

MEETING THE FUTURE

This one thing I do — I press toward the mark. PHILIPPIANS 3:13, 14

As we come to the close of another year, there are many who are fearful and a bit restless, about the days yet unborn. I have been reading the predictions of the politicians, the economists and the sociologists. Some are certain; some are reticent; some are reserved in their opinions about the coming year. The common thread appears to be a concern about the human relationships of men and nations. If they knew how men and nations were going to act they could make a better job of their prophecies.

It is this business of uncertainty that reveals afresh that we have been putting our trust in the wrong things. We are discovering that faith in ourselves, in our educational systems, in science, in international agreements and even in war, is not the foundation upon which to build for the future.

Where there is no faith in the future,
There is no power in the present.

Where are we to seek such confidence in faith for the days that lie ahead? I hope that we do not rely on the same sources that have disillusioned so many in this generation: Confidence in ourselves, our class, our colour, our political persuasions; these things have exploded and in the explosion our dreams have been shattered and our gods have fallen at our feet. We thought that the world of our making was good. We have discovered that it was good-for-nothing.

Let me bring you now to the source from which we must derive our strength, that will enable us to fashion for God and man, a better world. Stand for a little while in the presence of Paul. Try to catch from him the spirit that must be ours if we are to assert the reign of righteousness in our world.

What was the foundation upon which he built his life? What was the message he preached that stimulated such a response? Who was the person that transformed and fitted him for his task?

Let us look at the message of his text. It is the message that each of us should take with us as we enter into the new year. The first concept that arises is the decisiveness of the message. Here is a spiritual ultimatum. "This one thing I do." Paul was conscious of Christ's ownership of his life. You have heard it said of people that they lack decisiveness. Their minds are never made up. The action is never completed. You remember the words of Christ, "You cannot serve God and Mammon." You cannot sit on the fence. There is no middle to which you can cling.

There are things in our lives that we must be more decisive about. As we enter a new year, we should decide how we are going to live, to what use we intend to put this life that God has given. How are we going to use the gifts that God has given us? How are we going to use the opportunities that God has given us? How are we going to use the freedom that God has given us? This one thing we must do. We must make up our mind. We must be decisive. The only intelligent answer we can give to these questions is to decide in God's favour. "Why halt ye between two opinions", was an ancient cry. It is still relevant.

If we are going to be God's men and women let us get on with it. Let us put our hand to the plough and refuse to turn back or be turned back. There are wrongs to be righted. There are fires of illwill to be put out. There are inequalities in human relationships to be removed. There are struggles between class, creed and colour awaiting our service. Our decision in these matters will make us the kind of men and women that God is seeking to transform the world.

There is another important thought here. Our decisions give us our directions. Paul was sure on this. He had before him a mark. It was not reached — it was something he was striving for. He was big enough and brave enough to know that the road to righteousness is hard and only courageous souls can make their way.

Do you ever ask yourself: What direction am I going? In the Church we too must ask ourselves: What is our goal? What is our objective? What is the prize we seek? Like Paul, I too, must confess that our future belongs to the man who will make Christ the centre of his life. Only Christ is capable of transforming our selfishness into His service, our fear and anxiety into boldness and our blindness into vision. Only Christ can release it. Release in our lives the strength to endure the travail of the way. We do not need more warnings, creeds, dogmas, sermons. What we need is a will to get going.

The final thought of our text centres around dedication. Dedication is the one piece of equipment that we need as we face not only the past, but the present and future. I read the other day of a pilot who attacked Pearl Harbour. For many hours before the attack he actually slept in his plane. He explained, when asked, "Asleep or awake I must know how to act." Paul was in prison when he wrote these words. Can a man confined be so bold? Can a man surrounded by the enemy exercise such freedom? The answer is found in a life and a spirit that was dedicated. You remember it was Paul who said, "I can do all things through Christ."

As we enter the new year we must reflect upon some of the decisions that we must make. In what direction will we go? What dedication will we bring to our tasks? What is your decision to this question, "What think ye of Christ"? What direction will you go when you hear these words, "Follow thou me"? What dedication in service will you give your church and its work?

If you remove a violin string from its envelope it is free to curl in any direction. But a violin string is not made to curl, it is made for music and to produce music it must be attached to the violin and tuned correctly. With bow in hand the Master may then produce music. It is only then that the string is free to do that for which it was made. So it is with us. We are not free to do that for which we were created, until we have been brought under discipline — until we have been harnessed by the Eternal.

Here am I Lord, use me.

ACKNOWLEDGEMENT

As this book was in progress, a number of individuals have been most generous in sharing their time, expertise and knowledge.

I particularly offer thanks to Mrs. Ella Hutchison, Secretary of York Memorial Presbyterian Church, Rev. Winston Newman, Minister of York Memorial Presbyterian Church, Mr. Barry Penhale, Publisher, Natural Heritage/Natural History.

My special thanks to Gail Stacey, who in her usual expert fashion, prepared the manuscript with diligence and care.

Fifty-Two Sundays: From the Pulpit of the Padre was edited by Dr. Rowland's son, Barry D. Rowland. Mr. Rowland has two previous books to his credit: *The Padre* (Natural Heritage/Natural History, 1982); *The Maple Leaf Forever* (Natural Heritage/Natural History, 1987).

Cover Photograph.
This picture hung in the room occupied by David Parsons Rowland during his wartime ministry in Holland.

Sent to the Padre by the minister of the Dutch Reformed Church, the back of the photo carries the inscription "A token of remembrance of the Battle of Otterloo — May 16th, 1945".

Printed in the USA
CPSIA information can be obtained
at www.ICGtesting.com
JSHW012032140824
68134JS00033B/3017